D0504132

2·50

An Autobiography by
MORECAMBE & WISE

There's No Answer to That!!

An Autobiography by
MORECAMBE & WISE
with help from Michael Freedland

There's No Answer to That!!

Arthur Barker Limited London
A subsidiary of Weidenfeld (Publishers) Limited

Copyright © 1981 Eric Morecambe, Ernie Wise and
Michael Freedland

Published in Great Britain by
Arthur Barker Limited
91 Clapham High Street
London SW4 7TA

All rights reserved. No part of this publication may
be reproduced, stored in a retrieval system, or
transmitted, in any form or by any means,
electronic, mechanical, photocopying, recording or
otherwise, without the prior permission of the
copyright owner.

ISBN 0 213 16803 0

Designed by Behram Kapadia
Printed in Great Britain by
Butler & Tanner Ltd, Frome and London

Contents

Introduction
by Michael Freedland

Morecambe and Wise first came together as fifteen-year-olds, two Northern lads with almost as much cheek as talent, who didn't for a moment suspect that they wouldn't end up as stars.

Ernie (*né* Wiseman) began in show business first. The son of a railwayman from East Ardsley, a Yorkshire pudding's throw from Leeds, he first heard the sound of laughs and felt the vibrations of applause when he appeared in working men's clubs with his father in the mid 1930s. They were then called Carson and Kid (later amended to Bert Carson and His Little Wonder) and regaled the beer-drinking members of the clubs with a combination of comic patter and saccharine songs like 'Little Pal' and 'It's My Mother's Birthday Today' and such chirpy numbers as 'Let's Have a Tiddly at the Milk Bar'.

While all this high living was enriching Ernest Wiseman's experience, if not his pocket, across the Pennines at the seaside resort of Morecambe Eric Bartholomew was trying to convince his parents that his chances of becoming a notable scholar were rather less than maybe. Finally his mother, Mrs Sadie Bartholomew, got the message and saved enough to send him to dancing classes. It was, he now says, the single most important decision in his life. It gave him the wish to become an entertainer and in 1938 he entered a whole series of talent contests. When he won the contest at Hoylake, the prize was an audition with Jack Hylton – until lately one of the country's top band leaders and now an impresario whose very name makes entertainers doff their hats. Eric got his audition and at the same time a part in a discoveries show going the rounds called *Youth Takes a Bow*. This was presented by Bryan Michie, a much-respected personality in the discoveries business.

The show was a good move – with good money – £5 a week. Soon after Eric joined it in 1939, *Youth Takes a Bow* could also boast a performer who had already entertained on the wireless, played in the West End and who had changed his name from Ernest Wiseman to Ernie Wise. And he had what the Americans would call a good track record – he had played with Arthur Askey and Richard Murdoch earlier that year in the stage version of *Band Waggon*. That was good enough for him to be earning £2 a week more than Sadie's youngster Eric, who regarded Ernie as a star.

It was while working for Bryan Michie that Sadie had an idea about her son. If young Ernie thought it a good move to change his name, so should Eric. A fellow entertainer suggested she look to Jack Benny's screen henchman who had very successfully named himself after his home town, Rochester. 'Where do you come from?' he asked. 'Morecambe,' she said.

Eric and Ernie became friends, shared the same digs – at Sadie Bartholomew's suggestion – and when the show disbanded, decided (or at least Sadie suggested and then decided for them) that they should become a double act.

Needless to say, they didn't become overnight sensations. But what they did discover was that they liked each other and, more important, could work together. With that enthusiasm they auditioned for a new show opening at the Prince of Wales Theatre in the West End. *Strike a New Note* starred Sid Field, a name to be spoken in hushed tones of respect as the comedian's comedian. They didn't do much in the show. In fact, they were the proverbial understudies waiting in vain for a chance to go on. And they only did that, as a double act, twice.

But they were noticed – enough to get regular work on the wireless in the series *Youth Must Have its Fling*. To their delight, nobody suggested flinging them out, and Eric's local paper proudly recorded the work of the lad who had made good, telling jokes with his partner 'in the American style'. They had Abbott and Costello as their idols, and a not too knowledgeable listener to their patter might have

viii

assumed that they had come over smuggled in a Lend-Lease parcel.

The Government were under no such illusion, however, when war broke out. Ernie joined the Merchant Navy, but the only part of the world he saw in the course of that service was the stretch of water from Newcastle to London as he delivered coal on a barge. When Eric's turn for war service came, somebody in the Ministry of Labour brought the double act together again, albeit indirectly. If Ernie were going to deliver the coal, then Eric could cut it. The Minister, Ernest Bevin, had initiated a scheme for calling young men up to work in the mines, and Eric was honoured by being one of these 'Bevin Boys'. When a doctor became suspicious about his heart, though, he was invalided out. But Eric was one of those people who believed ill health was something that happened to other people, and from that moment on he barely gave the idea of a weak heart any thought. He suspected that he had been examined by a sympathetic doctor, for it must have been obvious that he didn't want to spend much time down a coal mine – hadn't he and his young partner Ernie Wise already become a double act?

Sadie Bartholomew, delighted to have her son back in Morecambe, decided that she would have to guide his career towards its next stage. She saw from an advertisement in *The Stage* that Edward Sanger, of the circus family, was planning a variety show alongside his usual entertainment in the big top. He was looking for a comedian. Sadie immediately rushed Eric along for an audition, but it was too late. The comedian's job had gone. There was still a vacancy for a feed, a straight man. 'Who is the comedian?' Sadie asked Sanger. 'You may have heard of him,' Sanger replied. 'The name's Ernie Wise.'

The pair were in business again. Ernie got £12 a week, Eric £10. But it didn't last long. There were times when they stood in the centre of the circus ring wearing dinner suits and gum-boots with nobody in the audience. When the show folded neither of them was sorry to say goodbye to the sort of life for which they were convinced they needed sawdust in either the blood or the head. They haunted agents' offices, this time with the idea that Eric would be the funny man.

Eric and Ernie invented 'Catch 22' before it became a household phrase. They were told they needed an agent before they could get work, yet they couldn't get work until they had an agent. Eventually they found one who booked them into the Walthamstow Palace, where they appeared as Morecambe and Wisdom because another comedian on the bill was called Wise – Vickie Wise. It was an inauspicious beginning.

They entertained the troops with ENSA and picked up spots whenever they could. In between they stayed at Sadie's house at Morecambe, sometimes having an overnight bus journey of up to eleven hours to get there. At the Windmill Theatre in Soho they trod the same path as Tony Hancock, Harry Secombe and Jimmy Edwards, those comics who bravely competed with the acres of bare flesh – which the customers had really paid their money to see – in the early years of their careers. Eric and Ernie later refused to allow their names to appear on the roll of honour at the Windmill, for in 1948 they had been sacked by Vivian Van Damm, and they didn't think the Windmill should be credited with discovering them. If perseverance is what gets a performer to the top, Eric and Ernie had a double dose of it. They recovered from the Windmill only to tumble again and again in variety theatres all over the country. And by the late forties there were not so many of those about.

Then they began to do better, working on the prestigious Moss Empire circuit and being helped in their struggles now they were married, both to dancers: Ernie to Doreen Blyth, whom he had met while working with Sanger's Circus and Eric to Joan Bartlett, who was in the chorus – she sang a bit, too – at the Edinburgh Empire.

The Wises set up house in Doreen's home town of Peterborough and Eric and Joan were, in the old showbiz tradition, on the road. They bought a caravan. And then, after too many demonstrations of Eric's total lack of mechanical expertise, took an old house in North London, converted it into flats and lived in one of them themselves.

Morecambe and Wise continued in variety for almost as long as there was such a thing, by the mid-1950s reaching the coveted number two spot to international entertainers like Lena Horne and Allan Jones. They were expanding their careers too. They appeared on radio, even having a series of their own, called *You're Only Young Once*.

In 1954 they got their first really big break – a chance to go on television; their own series, displaying a brand-new image on the virtually brand-new medium. The press response was amazing. 'How dare they put such mediocre talent on television!' said one critic.

'Definition of the week: television set – the box in which they buried Morecambe and Wise,' said another.

If they could survive that sort of thing, they thought, they could recover from anything.

In fact the programmes did get better – and when they returned to the variety stage, the pair could now be billed as 'Those Brilliant TV Comics, Morecambe and Wise'. They then did an ITV series with the pianist Winifred Atwell, and went to Australia with her. People began to sit up and take notice. Now, they thought, they were ready for another television series of their own – although a few months 'down under' meant that the public had forgotten who they were and they had to begin selling themselves again.

They did. On *Sunday Night at the London Palladium*, they earned £100 a show between them and ATV thought they were sufficiently interesting to give a half-hour spot to Morecambe and Wise on Thursday nights. By the end of that series they were almost accepted as television stars. It would take another batch of thirteen shows for that to happen. But they were good enough to be selected for the 1961 *Royal Variety Show*.

They had also seemingly made it to America – being featured on the famous Ed Sullivan television shows – although it has always remained a point of disappointment with them that they have never become anything like as big in America as they are at home. But Ed Sullivan did introduce them to a new public three thousand miles away from Morecambe Pier and when twenty years later, American television showed a retrospective of some of his best shows, the Morecambe and Wise programmes were among the ones chosen.

When they returned to England in 1962 they were topping the bill on stage and television with shows written for them by Dick Hills and Sid Green. Ernie and Doreen were happily settling in to a new home and Eric and Joan had started a family, a daughter called Gail and a son, Gary. In 1963 their show was number two in the TAM ITV ratings and they were voted the top Television Light Entertainment Personalities of the year by the Guild of TV Producers and Directors. They did twenty brilliant weeks at the North Pier, Blackpool. When they wanted to, Morecambe and Wise could earn fabulous sums in one-night stands at other variety theatres. These were so lucrative they called them 'bank raids'.

The Variety Club gave them their Silver Heart Award in 1964 and one top engagement followed another. Then, they switched to BBC TV for the best-produced and best-received series they had done to date. Eric and Ernie were working harder than ever, as though there were no tomorrow. For Eric there almost wasn't. In November 1968, while working at the Batley Variety Club, he felt ill. He stumbled into his car, drove off, and somewhere near Leeds asked a passing pedestrian to drive him on to the Leeds Royal Infirmary.

On the top of the showbiz world, it now seemed that Eric Morecambe was about to fall off. At forty-two he had had a heart attack. In one way it did him more good than all his years on television and those before. It helped establish one of the principal factors which singled out Morecambe and Wise from all the other showbiz double acts: the love they receive from their audiences. It is plain to see it when they perform in a television studio, even when they are rehearsing in an athletic club at Richmond-on-Thames. People see them and smile.

I smiled a lot at the club after their rehearsals – as, day after day, they talked about their lives and the brand of show business of which they are undoubtedly the masters.

We began with that first heart attack.

1

An Unexpected Break

ERIC: on 7 November 1968 I was taken to Leeds Infirmary.

ERNIE: How long were you there?

ERIC: About five feet ten inches. Two weeks actually.

ERNIE: His heart attack came as a complete surprise. There was no warning. I just couldn't believe what had happened. I got the phone call at one o'clock in the morning in the hotel in Wakefield. It was the ward sister.

All she said was, 'Your partner has had a heart attack and he's in the hospital.'

I didn't sleep the rest of the night.

ERIC: He couldn't sleep the rest of the night because he was trying to get in touch with this insurance fellow.

ERNIE: It was too late. It was the thirty days. There's an interesting story about that: a few years before, my insurance broker had said to me, 'You know, as a member of a partnership it would be a good idea for you to insure yourself against anything happening to your partner.'

I felt a bit guilty about that. I said, 'Oh, I don't know. I don't like insuring that sort of situation.'

But he was insistent. He said it was a good idea and it would give me a guaranteed income if anything ever happened to Eric. So I agreed and took out a policy. I think it cost me about £200 a year, and I did it for two years. When it came due for renewal for the third year, I said, 'I keep paying this premium but it's a waste of money.' Eric was fine, so I cancelled it.

About a week later he had his heart attack. It sounds like a set-up story, doesn't it?

ERIC: I didn't insure Ernie. He's too fit. And I don't insure myself, either.

ERNIE: Eric didn't *look* sick, even then. I went to see him the day after his attack. He'd been on holiday and he was tremendously tanned. Joan was there too. I didn't know what to expect, so I went into the room somewhat sheepishly. But there he was in the oxygen tent, sitting up and as black and as bright as a button. It seemed as though that heart attack had done him the world of good. He looked fantastic. There was a monitor screen bleeping at the side of his bed, but I don't think he was aware of how serious it was. We didn't let on. He sat there looking at us and we looked at him. He didn't know much about it.

ERIC: No. Not until the doctor told me. All I knew was that I felt a tremendous constriction when breathing and a lot of pain. I thought I had something wrong with the lungs and was sure a pill and a couple of days in hospital would cure it. Then the doctor said, 'You've had a mild heart attack.'

ERNIE: The worst part was collecting all his things from the Selby Fork Motel outside Leeds where he had been staying. We always stay at separate hotels because we have different tastes. People may think we live together in that flat in our shows, but the time has come to reveal all: we don't share the same double bed. We do, though, have a means of communicating that some think is uncanny. I have heard people say, 'It's in the eyes; the way you look at each other.' Well, all the time Eric was in hospital, the communication was less direct. But we each knew what the other felt. Anyway, I picked up all his things, his clothes and shoes and all that . . . wigs.

ERIC: You got quite a lot of money for them, didn't you?

ERNIE: Yes, quite a lot.

ERIC: Funny, we laugh at that now – well, I do anyway. I laugh at the illness – although every now and again I am inclined to think, Why me? What have *I* done? Am I so bad that I have to suffer this?

ERNIE: Jimmy, the fellow who ran the club at Batley where we were appearing, was broken-hearted. He was sold out. We'd been there for almost two weeks.

ERIC: I didn't have to worry what my illness was doing to Ernie's career. You can count on your hand who your real friends are, and I consider Ernie a real friend. I know he considers me one, too. If there were difficulties in life there would be no problems between us.

ERNIE: You'll get nothing from me!

ERIC: Frankly, I don't think it would be easy for us to work together if we weren't friends.

ERNIE: I don't agree. I think we *could* still work together.

ERIC: Yes, but there would be something missing. People look at us and say, 'They like each other, you can see that.'

ERNIE: Everybody probes the social background, but we're totally different. Eric has a family and I don't.

ERIC: He's got a strict mother-in-law, you see. So no children.

ERNIE: He has school holidays, I don't.

ERIC: I say to Ernie, 'I can't go on holiday or abroad until the youngest has had his holidays from school' – and we work it out for ourselves from there.

ERNIE: We are in the lucky position of being independent of each other.

ERIC: But that's after forty years! And forty years of hard work. The reason I had the heart attack was because of the hard work.

ERNIE: Don't forget we are a very compact unit, the two of us. Morecambe and Wise together are a force to be reckoned with. Split it up and the whole picture changes tremendously. You would have to start all over again. Eric Morecambe and Ernie Wise don't exist on their own. It's Morecambe and Wise as the bookable proposition.

ERIC: For guaranteed money. After the heart attack, I was in the fortunate position of being able to turn round and say, 'Well, if I don't have to work for three months, then I won't work for six months. I can be twice as fit if I go without work for twice as long.' I doubled the time off work that the doctors had insisted on. It seemed the sensible thing to do.

ERNIE: It's true that we've never been under financial pressure. Hardly ever, except right at the beginning in the early days. Six months off? It didn't seem that long.

ERIC: My heart attack struck when I was doing the act. The only thing I remember was whispering to Ernie, 'Let's get off. Let's keep it short.'

I knew I wasn't well, but what was actually wrong never occurred to me. The audience didn't know. Yet that's what it was – I was having a heart attack.

Getting over it was in its way harder than the initial pain. What worried me most was not that I wouldn't get out of the oxygen tent alive, but that I'd end up a chronic invalid, perhaps in a wheelchair, waited on hand and foot. It got to the point where I would be frightened to face people on my left side – because I thought that if anyone touched me there, I'd have another attack. So I just looked at them from the right. It was Joan who, as always, put things into their perspective for me. One day she came out with it: 'You've got to go out to work,' she said.

I knew she was right and that I couldn't wrap myself in cotton-wool. Easing off was one thing, packing up altogether was something different.

We had just started working for the BBC before I went into hospital. They had offered us the chance of working in colour, which ATV had refused to do.

ERNIE: Lew Grade wouldn't compromise on that. He said, 'You'll have colour when I say you have colour.' We wanted colour as soon as we could, so we left ATV that day. Bill Cotton came to us and said he would give us colour, and of course we would be backed up by the BBC's prestige.

ERIC: They were absolutely fantastic about the six months convalescence. As soon as I was better, Bill Cotton was happy for us to pick up where we had left off. They allowed us a month to do three 45-minute shows instead of the week we usually took for one half-hour one. Actually, I've always thought we were conned into those, since we were originally booked for half-hour shows and they never paid us any extra for the longer ones. But they were a good series, and they were good for us.

ERNIE: At that time we had Dick Hills and Sid Green scriptwriting for us – or at least we thought we had.

ERIC: Then we found that they had gone to work in America.

ERNIE: I learned that little piece of information on the flight from New York to Barbados. The chief steward walked the whole way down the aircraft to tell me. 'I see your writers have left you,' he

4

began. I didn't know what he was talking about until he said, 'Hills and Green have gone to America.' He had heard it on the radio before leaving London. I hadn't.

ERIC: The first thing I knew about it was a telephone call soon after my heart attack. The press rang and said, 'What are you going to do now that your writers have left?'

ERNIE: You could argue that they should have been put on a retainer.

ERIC: Yes, from their point of view. But we were big friends and if they had told us on the phone they had an American offer of work we might have gone with them. Now it's all bridge under the waters of the River Kwai but then we were up a gum tree, without a writer.

That was how Eddie Braben came on the scene. Bill Cotton asked us in a lift at the Television Centre:

'How do you fancy Eddie?'

I said, 'Send me a photograph and I'll tell you.' No, our immediate thought was: if he writes as well for us as he does for Ken Dodd, then the answer must be 'yes'. We dropped him a line, and Eddie came down to see us. There was an initial problem with the sort of material we wanted. He said, 'I don't do sketches. I only write jokes.'

ERNIE: But we knew he had an original mind and when Eddie did a joke it was one you'd not heard before.

ERIC: We simply said, 'If you can write original jokes, you can write original sketches.' We encouraged him and gave him ideas for formats from which he came forth like lotus blossom. He was absolutely fantastic. He wrote with tremendous ease at his home in Liverpool and sent the scripts from there down to us in London. He works to the same pattern today. The ease of things helped us tremendously. We were doing thirteen shows a year, or perhaps fourteen, with the BBC, but not doing any theatres at all.

ERNIE: But soon we were. They seemed so easy and brought us so much cash that 'bank raids' was the obvious name for them.

ERIC: In 1970 we did the first four of the 45-minute *Morecambe and Wise Shows*. The money really wasn't such an important factor. What we wanted was backing and production facilities. In exchange for the right studio back-up I would have been quite willing to earn less cash. It's great that the public thinks we make up our shows as we go along – perhaps that's the gift we have – but it isn't anything like as easy as that. We need to have a television company willing to spend money on making the shows look like that.

The BBC gave us what we wanted. In the second year we did a couple of bank raids, and in the third we did four or five; eventually we were doing more bank raids than television – we did four in four months. Then came a Christmas special and a series of thirteen for BBC TV. It's a psychological thing – once you've done the first show after you've been ill, you're all right. It's just like driving after an accident. Or flying again after a plane crash.

ERNIE: Do those planes ever crash?

ERIC: Only once. We do enjoy the luxury of being able to take our time. Even if the television companies find it expensive.

ERNIE: I remember Bill Cotton saying at a conference at Montreux, 'Gentlemen, you realize, of course, that comedies, like all shows, are getting terribly expensive. If a joke is too expensive, you can't do it. I'm sure Ernie Wise would agree with that.'

I said, 'No, I don't. If it gets a big laugh, I don't care what it costs.'

ERIC: That's a comic's point of view.

ERNIE: Of course, you mustn't spend a lot of money on a routine that's not good. If you do that, you're in trouble. If it's a disaster they won't want you to do it again. The great thing is that if we want to go to, say, Norway to make a programme, we have the back-up to let us go. Or if we want a studio for two whole days, even though it would be expensive to buy studio time for that sort of period, I like to think we can get it. And the BBC were not holding us back when Eric was ready.

ERIC: The only real difficulty with having our shows fifteen minutes longer was that we had more to learn and more to do.

ERNIE: The big problem is time. When we first look at a sketch, our usual reaction is 'It's too long.' So we edit it down to what we think is a good running time and, if it happens to be very funny, we play it for all it's worth. If it gets the big laughs, it becomes long again.

ERIC: On the other hand, when we *have* to cut down a sketch from eleven to eight minutes, it feels as if we're losing blood. There certainly was a great advantage for us in only having to do one show a month. It set a new pattern for us.

ERNIE: We just spread it out. And you know what happens when you spread it out and don't do as much work? The price goes up.

6

ERIC: And more work comes in, funnily enough. Work that we normally wouldn't have got in the first place. When you turn things down, they want you even more. We've looked after our money. We're not rich men, but we've invested as well as we know how, with our limited knowledge. We've not had all that marvellous expert advice that stars are supposed to get.

ERNIE: We've never done any of the clever things that people seem to do. We just pay our taxes.

ERIC: Businessmen who have earned the money we have earned would be millionaires by now – or broke.

ERNIE: We've never gone to Australia for twelve months to avoid a tax year or anything like that.

ERIC: No, we don't let that come into it. We only work when we want to work now. Heart trouble made up my mind on that.

ERNIE: Before 1968 we were working much, much more.

ERIC: If we heard there were twenty people wanting to see us, we would go and play to them, and if they gave us the right money, we would perform. Anywhere, just so long as the deal was right.

ERNIE: Before Eric had his heart attack we were lined up to do an Ed Sullivan show in New York and three spots for the *Royal Variety Show*. In the event all of it went by the board, but I remember getting a telegram from Bernard Delfont after we turned down the royal show. It was a long, long telegram: 'I need you madly,' it said. Then he phoned and and said, 'Dear boys, I need you.'

ERIC: He really pleaded. 'You've got to do this for me,' he said. We refused because it meant finding new material. We had a show to do in Glasgow; we were doing the night-clubs and had to find enough for the three programmes in America. It would have been impossible taking on the *Royal Variety Show* at that time.

ERNIE: You know what our business is like when everybody wants you.

ERIC: Within three weeks.

ERNIE: After that, you can't get yourself arrested. I think the only time we had had a similar crisis was when we were doing pantomime at Manchester. It wasn't so bad because we already knew the pantomime, and didn't have to rehearse it; we'd done it the year before. But no matter how well you know a pantomine, it can be a pretty tiring way to earn a living. Then we had to do a *Sunday Night at the Palladium* television show. I knew Eric wasn't very well. He felt his

7

legs were tired, and the act didn't get much of a response. As we came off, Eric said, 'This must be the worst bloody act we've ever done.' The trouble was we still had our throat mikes on and the whole of England heard him say it.

ERIC: I'd had a couple of injections that night and they dragged me down a bit. There used to be a stage manager at the Palladium called Jack Matthews, a lovely man, who is dead now. He had got to the age that we are fast approaching now and his speed had gone a little bit. We had a routine that had a lot of things going on – lifts and circles going round, pianos coming in at the same time. But it was all a half a minute late and there was a chap chipping us from the audience: 'Why don't you stand on your heads?'

'Where are you from?' I asked. 'Australia?' But we didn't get a laugh.

ERNIE: I fainted.

ERIC: That's the only laugh he did get. I used to ring my mother and father after every television show. The next day I rang them in Morecambe and asked what they thought of the show, knowing both that it hadn't been great and that I had told the nation that it was the worst one we had ever done.

My mother said, 'Oh, I suppose it was all right.'

I replied, 'Well, it's one of those things.'

But she wasn't having that. 'It's all right for you down there, doing these shows that are not very good, but I've got to go to the shops in Morecambe. It was so bad that I won't be able to go there this week. I'll have to do my shopping in Lancaster. What was the matter with you, were you drunk?'

And that wasn't all.

ERNIE: As we walked on in our first opening of this highly success-ful pantomime in Manchester on Monday night someone from the audience shouted, 'What happened last night?'

ERIC: You don't feel great after that.

ERNIE: On the one hand, you're highly successful, and on the other, the big show has gone wrong. Nevertheless, the house was full that night and we had to show them we could still be terrific, despite all that had misfired.

ERIC: There was a mark against us. But it was because the pressure had built up and up. It was a case of everybody wanting us and our not being able to say no. 'Just pop in,' they'd say, 'it'll only be an hour' or 'it'll only be twenty minutes.' And we always said yes. We didn't realize we couldn't do it. Today, I suppose it would all depend on who was offering the twenty minutes. If Sophia Loren said, 'Could you spare me twenty minutes ...?'

ERNIE: When you get on the treadmill of tiredness you've got to be careful. This is where the danger of the *Valley of the Dolls* comes in. We've never started taking the pink and blue pills but, under that pressure, anyone might resort to them. And if you never catch up on the tiredness it causes, you become very irritable. With the BBC working with us and Eddie Braben writing our shows, we now had a chance to decide what sort of life we were going to make for ourselves.

ERIC: And I had no doubt what I was going to do: with the doctor's permission, it was going to be back to work as hard as before but not so often.

That cliché about it being an ill wind – and I'm not talking about the producer – was true with us. We joined the BBC in late 1968 and we only did one series before I was taken ill. But it was through my illness that we got the idea for the shows that really made us a huge success, the 45-minute programmes working with major guest stars. And that one, like all good ideas, came right out of the blue.

2

Be Our Guests

ERIC: The bigger the star the better the show – that's the way we look at it now. The morning after the show it's Ernie and I who are remembered, even if we didn't do very much ourselves.

ERNIE: Talking of the celebrities on our shows, I don't think we'll ever forget Peter Cushing, our first guest.

ERIC: He always wore white gloves in rehearsal – he was playing King Arthur in Ernie's *Knights of the Round Table*.

ERNIE: It was a Braben idea, incidentally, turning me into a playwright. Another early one was my *Elizabeth I*, played by Dame Flora Robson. One of the lines in that play was, 'Let Philip sail with the Spanish fleet.'

And Dame Flora replied, 'You need men. Have you got the chaps?'

'Yes,' I said, 'it's these tights.'

We found those ridiculous exchanges really worked. And Dame Flora said she actually enjoyed being on the show – and not just because it made managements realize she was still alive! She was a lovely guest, and when we did some bank raids at Brighton she came to see us every time; afterwards she always walked up I don't know how many flights of stairs to the dressing-room.

ERIC: She was in the queue when we came to Brighton to promote one of our books. I said, 'Don't buy the book, we can send you one at half the price.' But she bought one just the same, and of course we signed it for her.

ERNIE: The routine of our guests never getting their money began with our first guest, as did our being rude to them. The worst line we had for Peter Cushing was, 'Are you going to bite my neck before you leave?' It got a good laugh and Eddie Braben has built on that ever since. And it has become a running joke that we never pay people; we are always being asked, 'When are you going to pay Peter?'

ERIC: The continuing theme of our shows is your brilliant and famous actor trying desperately hard but hating every second because Ernie and I are ruining it.

ERNIE: You have to match the words with the great presence.

ERIC: We appear to be doing everything in one of Ernie's plays to the best of our ability, but always getting the words slightly wrong – not unlike the cast in a fifth-rate amateur dramatic society. For instance, when I had a sheet over my head playing the ghost in *Hamlet* I wore my glasses over it.

'I can't see without the glasses,' I said.

ERNIE: We had Eric Porter in the early days as well. He actually danced on the show. We did the song and dance 'If They Could See Me Now' from *Sweet Charity* and he learned it like an actor, step by step by step, as though he were remembering dialogue. He was in a show with Bill Franklyn and Edward Woodward, playing *The Three Musketeers*.

We had another in 1970 with a marvellous mixture of celebrities – Felix Aylmer, Sir Michael Redgrave, Robin Day, Flora Robson again and Barbara Murray. The idea was that there was a wonderful play what I'd wrote, but there was no way any of them was going to play in it, because Eric was to be the star.

The sketch began when I phoned Flora and she said, 'Will your partner Eric be there?' I said yes and she said, 'I'm afraid I've broken my leg.' There were a whole lot of calls like that. Finally, I sent it to Barbara Murray.

ERIC: By that time Ernie had tumbled to the reaction of stars and he told Barbara, 'Don't worry, Eric won't be in it.

She said, 'Well, if he won't, then I'm not doing it.'

Once we had had Flora and Barbara, Sir Michael, Peter Cushing and Eric Porter, all very big at the time, the pattern was set. Of course, everything's done for charity. The Eric Morecambe charity. I don't even let the stars know that I appreciate their acting.

Somebody says, 'I'm at the National,' and I say, 'Well, I saw the race and I didn't notice you anywhere' or 'Oh yes, you came in third, I lost a fortune on you.'

What we really like to do is to get hold of a star and present him in a totally surprising way. We might get someone like Warren Mitchell, for instance, and ask him to play the accordion. Nobody has heard he's a great accordion player – which, as it happens, he isn't. But if he was and he'd never done it on television before, that would be great for us. Or Robert Robinson. Wouldn't it be marvellous if he really played a fair oboe? Or if Trevor McDonald liked to impersonate Al Jolson? That was how we got Angela Rippon. She was sitting next to me at a Variety Club lunch and I asked her quite casually, 'Do you do anything else other than read the news?'

She said, 'Well, I used to be a ballet dancer. I still like dancing and I enjoy movement and things like that.'

So I said, 'If Ernie and I ever get a good idea for you, would you come and do our Christmas show with us?'

And she said she'd love to.

Don't forget, we never get these big stars and push custard pies into their faces. We either treat them rough verbally and have no respect for them, or we're over-respectful – which is worse.

ERNIE: We puncture them, but they are big enough stars to take it. Everyone knows it's a joke – and at our expense, not theirs.

But surprise is always the best recipe for finding out stars' secret sides. We always do the asking ourselves, in a discreet way. You'd be surprised the background that some of them have. Rex Harrison plays the clarinet. John Mills was a dancer. We can be surprised ourselves.

On one of our shows we had Paul Anka who wrote 'My Way'. I remember that he wore his stetson all through rehearsal. Also there was Patricia Lambert who used to be our principal girl and who came straight from the light opera stage. She was the Sleeping Beauty in our pantomime. I used to carry her off stage every night saying, 'The princess has pricked her finger.' Believe me, it's the sort of line that can be frightening ... it's so easy to muddle the words. Eventually she surprised me by getting a bit too heavy. She nearly killed me!

ERIC: We would like Anna Ford on the show, but the problem was getting permission from ITN. I'd love to get hold of Sophia Loren –

ERNIE: Who wouldn't?

ERIC: I'll rephrase that. I'd love to have Sophia Loren –

ERNIE: So would I.

ERIC: I'd love Sophia Loren –

ERNIE: So would I.

ERIC: Sophia Loren would be good.

ERNIE: She'd be great as Eliza Doolittle in *My Fair Lady*. We would simply tell her to talk in Italian throughout the show, then we'd say, 'You haven't got it quite right, dear.' You've got to have a vehicle – preferably a truck – for these people, otherwise they just become straight men and women who end up apologizing.

Of course, you can't always predict the public's reaction to a guest. Another difficulty is that very often stars use other people as middlemen or buffers to say no for them. I know – we've done it ourselves. We're asked to go on shows and we sometimes say we'd love to, then we ask our agent to say no for us, but say it's *his* idea.

ERIC: We used to be nervous with our guest stars in the early days.

ERNIE: Juliet Mills was one of the first ladies we had. She doesn't look any different now, still charming and lovely. . . .

ERIC: Of course, I may not be living with the times, but I didn't enjoy hearing her say on *Parkinson*, 'We were pissed all night!'

ERNIE: She's grown up now. I've never seen a daughter look so much like her father – it's incredible. She's taller than he is, though.

ERIC: Who isn't?

ERNIE: We like these important actors to suggest ideas for us, and John Mills was typical of many guest stars – all they want to do is be funny. Then we settle in and rehearse. After three days they start taking out the gags because they're losing their nerve. They come in thinking it's all going to be a hoot and only later do they realize that it's a serious job. We might do it our way, but it's serious all right – and sincere.

ERIC: They say, 'You know that joke? Well, I don't think I'll say it.'

So I tell them, 'Okay, *I'll* say it.' I'll grab anything. One laugh and you see the worried look on their faces.

We were doing an escape film with John Mills which I was going to call *Colditz*. I'd just thought it up.

'But I've already done the film,' he said.

'Never saw it,' I said and denied any knowledge of such a movie.

I haven't yet worked with a guest star – and we've had some very, very good guests – who hasn't shown a sign of nerves when they first come on. You always see it in the eyes – that slightly vacant look which shows they're thinking.

ERNIE: But we don't try to put them at ease.

ERIC: No. That's their problem.

ERNIE: On the other hand, we don't like to get them uptight.

ERIC: When we started rehearsing with John Mills he put a moustache on and, as the show got nearer, added a kilt.

ERNIE: He was acquiring a character.

ERIC: But he was hiding. All actors have to hide. They can't play themselves. The only thing that Ernie and I do *is* play ourselves. But real actors find it very difficult. The classic case is Frank Finlay. The first time we asked him to do a show with us, he had just completed Casanova, which was an enormous success and made him a star. He said he'd love to do it. We told him that the idea was that he'd play himself first and then go into our version of the Casanova story. The gag was that a drunk would walk on stage and just as we were ordering him off, he'd say, 'My name is Frank Finlay', and get a round of applause.

A quarter of the way through the opening routine Frank sidled up to Ernie and whispered, 'I've had enough of this, I'd like to go home. Take me off, please.'

ERNIE: He couldn't play himself. It was whispered very quietly into my ear, but it is there on tape and the viewers might just have heard it. And yet when we got him in the Casanova bit, he was superb. He had a classic line: 'I have a long-felt want . . .' The trouble was, too many people laughed. That was the scene where we had a bed with four balls on top of it. I said, 'By Jove, it's cold today', and they all dropped. That really was basic. In scenes like that, Frank was absolutely brilliant. He was playing a part. We asked Albert Finney to appear once.

ERIC: He was playing for Preston North End at the time.

ERNIE: He said, 'No. I find it difficult to play myself.'

So I said, 'Who are you now, then?' But on the whole actors can't play themselves; the only one I know who can is Glenda Jackson. I do understand why they find it so difficult. Once I get on the suit I'm wearing on the show and a bit of make-up too, I'm somebody else. Whatever that means.

ERIC: We've always told our guest stars at the beginning what we want from them. Most comics give their guests nothing to do and make them look like idiots. We don't want that to happen to ours. If we can, we like to give them a lot of good lines. If they get a laugh, then it's in the *Morecambe and Wise Show* they're getting it, and people say, 'Did you see Vanessa Redgrave with Morecambe and Wise?'

ERNIE: We've never put anyone down. We're dealing with big, big stars. So if I were to say to Flora Robson, 'That last film you made wasn't a patch on one of my plays', nobody would take it seriously. Certainly, she wouldn't take offence. It's so patently ridiculous. And then I'd say to her, 'I could have written something greater and made you into a big star.' It's so silly, that it's funny!

ERIC: But we couldn't do it to Mavis Tittle, who nobody's ever heard of. If I told her – and she doesn't exist, I must emphasize – 'I saw you in your last film and it was bloody awful', I'd be hurting her. We always say to our guests, 'You've got to give that look, the one that says, what have I let myself in for?'

It's our female guest stars who seem to get people talking most. There are two ladies who work with us more than anybody else – both lovely people, Glenda Jackson and Hannah Gordon. Hannah's last Christmas show with us was her fourth. Nobody else would ask a guest that many times, but we know when we are on to a good thing – and Hannah's a good thing whichever way you look at her. There's a good mix with us. We like her and she likes us, and she likes the shows too. There are no problems. If the sketch is bad, she doesn't care. There's chemistry there.

ERNIE: Glenda regards being on our show as a plus. She doesn't do it for the money.

ERIC: No. She's someone we couldn't buy. At the beginning we didn't believe it could possibly work. I remember when we first had Glenda on the show in 1971.

ERNIE: She played Cleopatra for us. It turned into one of those magic moments. The actress who had played Elizabeth I from a teenager to an old woman and won all sorts of awards now played Cleopatra for laughs. And she carried a Roman-style banner supporting Luton Town FC.

It was as a result of appearing with us that she was offered the part in *A Touch of Class*. That established her as the top cinema comedy star. Mel Frank saw Glenda on our show and offered her the role that won the Academy Award.

15

ERIC: We treated her – anyway, we tried to – with a certain amount of awe when we first met her. After all, she was a very famous lady. I saw her when Joan and I were on holiday with a friend from Harpenden. She was the first person I bumped into at the hotel outside Salisbury where she was making *Triple Echo*. Later, we went on location with her and attended her last-night party. It made a marvellous holiday – and I caught some fish as well.

ERNIE: We did a sketch with her in the flat, and then came her Cleopatra. It all started when we saw in the paper that Glenda wanted to do comedy. Johnny Ammonds simply rang her up.

ERIC: I took a bet with him that she wouldn't do it. But she did. Of course, you can't always be sure that a sketch will be funny.

ERNIE: There was the one when I was singing in full Highland outfit while Eric appeared with a huge salmon plus a whole lot of dead rabbits and other things hanging off him. While I was singing Eric lit his pipe, threw down the match – and a mass of flames went up my kilt. We did a quickie of that, and put it on tape.

ERIC: We had that kilt gag quite a while, and before I saw the tape I said, 'I'll stake my reputation that none of it will be any good.' But it turned out the best quickie we'd ever done – and the audience thought so too when they saw it.

ERNIE: Some of the best situations we've dreamed up have been a kind of blackmail. Like trying to persuade Glenda in the flat sketch to appear as Cleopatra. The gag was that we recorded our conversation, hiding the machine under the table, and Glenda regaled us with all sorts of terrible stories about people. Then, when she said she wasn't going to do our Cleopatra, we simply played back the worst things she'd said.

ERIC: Glenda took it just as seriously as we did. Before she went on she asked, 'Am I doing this right? Is there anything you want to tell me about the character I'm playing in the sketch?'

All I said was, 'Just make it louder and faster.'

So she went on and she played it loud and fast. She was great. When she won her Oscar in *A Touch of Class* we sent her a telegram. We wrote, 'Stick with us and you'll get another award.' She came back on the show and did a Queen Victoria sketch. Then she made another film and got another award!

ERNIE: Actually, we felt a little bit insulted after Mel Frank called her. He said, 'Gee, that girl can do comedy.' He didn't offer *us* anything! Glenda's a wonderful actress. She can play a dowdy old spinster as well as a glamorous sex image. Quite incredible.

ERIC: I find her an extremely sexual lady.

ERNIE: We went to see her in a play in London. She wasn't very pleased that we did. She knew we'd be upset by all the four-letter words in it.

ERIC: I must emphasize that we never give our guests rubbish to do. We don't make them straight men and straight women. They have an identity. We try to give them lines that perpetuate that identity – but which don't do us any harm either. Imagine Glenda reading a terrible line like 'It's in the play what you wrote.' But nobody will forget she said it.

Our experience with Vanessa Redgrave was a little more serious. She played Josephine to Ernie's Napoleon – and always worked according to the rules. When she finished at 12.30 she finished.

ERNIE: Once she said to me, 'Let's face it, you don't own the BBC', and I said, 'Well, the way we're going, we will.'

ERIC: But she is a major star. She's a very tall lady, a foot taller than I am. To make her look even taller, Ernie was in flats when we worked with her.

We said, 'You will play the part of Josephine.' And she said, 'Okay, I'll be right back.' At which point I said, 'She's tall enough to play in goal!' That was a great line, one that you remember.

ERNIE: She's the complete actress, you see. The first morning she came, she didn't glam herself up or anything for us. She just wore a long coat and she had a big handbag.

ERIC: It wasn't a handbag, it was an attic ... to lift it up you'd need a truss. I've had worse digs than that handbag.

ERNIE: The classic situation happened on the day we were going to have our picture taken for the press. She said, 'Oh, I wish you could have told me. I would have put some eye make-up on.' She had on this long coat and her very wild hair, but on the show she looked a million dollars –

ERIC: All green and crinkled –

ERNIE: And her skin was like a peach –

ERIC: All covered with fuzz. She looked like a million dollars, but a lot of it was in loose change. She had an hour-glass figure, but the time was running out.

ERNIE: She was wearing a going-away dress – it looked like part of it had already left. Oh yes, she was the perfect professional.

ERIC: One of the problems is that actors sometimes work too hard at being funny. In our 1980 series, Hugh Paddick, who is a very, very good performer, seemed quite subdued during the first two or three run-throughs. He'd got the voice and he acted beautifully, playing a pouf. But he was a bit shy about doing it.

I told him, 'Go as wild as you want to.' He'd never had that said to him before. All the other comics he'd worked with had said, 'Hold on, don't overdo that because it's too funny.' They were frightened that he would steal the show from them. But we don't look at it like that. The more laughs he gets, the more laughs the show gets. And the more talked about it is. Nobody is going to turn round and say Hugh Paddick wiped the floor with Morecambe and Wise. They're going to say, 'Did you see Hugh Paddick in the *Morecambe and Wise Show*?' and that's good, that's marvellous.

ERNIE: I must say we have built up super relationships with almost all our guests. Michelle Dotrice was a darling. We did a number with her called 'A Right Way to do it, A Wrong Way to do it', the really gutsy Shirley Bassey song. The trouble was she had a very light voice, so we had to change the whole concept of the tune. But it still worked. And we did *Lady Chatterley's Lover* with her.

ERIC: I've never been the same since, as a matter of fact.

ERNIE: That's right.

ERIC: I rolled over and threw my leg up in the air and that was the start of everything.

ERNIE: It never came down, did it?

ERIC: Good God, agonies.

ERNIE: We did it at that old house.

ERIC: That was great. I like location work and, unfortunately, we have very few opportunities for it. I mean the sort of location work where the landlord takes you in and says, 'Would you like a sherry, sir?' Oh yes, that sort I like, not your standing-in-the-bloody-freezing-cold locations. I don't want to know about that.

ERNIE: Diana Rigg gave us a lot of fun on location. I think she is one of the most beautiful women of our time, a very experienced artist, very professional. We went out to Banbury to do our number with her. It was in the main hall of a castle. She played Nell Gwynn, a superb sight in a dress that made the oranges blush. But when she took a look at herself in the mirror – ginger wig and all – all she could say was, 'Good Lord, I'm Danny La Rue!'

I remember lying on the bed with her as we rehearsed, doing the same scene again and again. 'I don't know what I'm going to tell my wife when I get back,' I said.

'What do you mean?' she asked.

So I told her: 'I'll have to say "I'm sorry I'm late, dear, but all day I've been going up and down on the bed with Diana Rigg."'

ERIC: That's a round of applause in itself.

ERNIE: It was at the end of that scene when Diana, Eric and I threw ourselves on to the bed, which then flew up into the wall. As it went up, you could see that the under side said 'That's All, Folks', like the end of a Tom and Jerry cartoon.

ERIC: Working with people like Diana, you get to know quite a lot about them. In fact, nothing is nicer than getting our guest stars to talk to us while we're having our pea soup and buns. They tell stories about their careers that are not just fascinating, but are as funny as any Eddie Braben script. Gordon Jackson was the co-star on that show, playing the butler to Diana Rigg's Nell Gwynn.

ERNIE: He's a lovely man. I remember he was doing an advert at the time, all about putting it in the Trustee Savings Bank.

ERIC: And you gave him a tip.

Robert Morley gave us a few tips too – about horses and about remembering which one of us was who. Robert decided that the taller half was the one with the longer name, Eric Morecambe. The shorter one was the one with the short name – but Wise.

ERNIE: Our favourite story about Robert is the one that illustrates his love of food – which is not difficult to appreciate from his size. He came to see us at the rehearsal studios we used at Delgano Way, a beautiful place backing on to Wormwood Scrubs. We started to rehearse at about ten or ten-thirty. By the time it got to about half-past twelve we could see he was getting restive. Finally he threw his hands in the air and asked, 'What are we going to do now, dear boys? Where do we go to eat?'

We said, 'It's all in there', and pointed to our sandwiches. We could see from his expression that this was sheer blasphemy.

'Sandwiches? Sandwiches? Isn't there a restaurant we could go to round the corner?' The way he asked sounded rather pitiful.

'No,' we replied, 'we always just bring in a few sandwiches and have a cup of tea and some pea soup.'

He was clearly sorry he'd signed the contract. He thought he was going to be whipped off to the Savoy. You could see his mind ticking over. '*I* will arrange to bring lunch tomorrow,' he said.

The next day, he came to rehearsal apparently with nothing more than a bottle of wine. I remember it well, South African rosé.

ERIC: Obviously, it was something he'd acquired from British Airways.

ERNIE: Of course, *we* hadn't brought anything that day because he promised to bring in the food. It was one o'clock and all we could do was stare at the bottle of rosé. And then, at five past one, a very well-dressed, handsome chauffeur knocked on the door and walked in carrying a heavy package. Robert had actually ordered a hamper from Fortnum and Mason containing six boxed lunches.

ERIC: And had it brought in a Rolls. Incredible! It cost him more than he got for doing the show.

ERNIE: He really did it in style, smoked salmon, the lot. We only drank his wine to make him feel comfortable.

ERIC: Mind you, he only did it once. It didn't become a dirty habit.

ERNIE: And we didn't pick up the relay stick! We went back to the sandwiches again. Reluctantly but proudly. We spent hours arguing and talking with Robert. He's a great talker, never gets the needle, doesn't lose his temper. He's fun and very intelligent.

ERIC: And everything wobbles when he smiles.

ERNIE: I remember he always used to lean on me when we were rehearsing – because I came under his elbow. Consequently, whenever we made an entrance together, I felt like a crutch. We occasionally meet him at a racecourse. Then he always seems a totally different personality, very different. He is a big gambler and when it comes to the horses he is very serious. He has given me a couple of good tips.

ERIC: Like inviting him back on the show.

What we admire in the great stage actors is their ability to learn lines so easily. Those fellows are so positive. When you give them a script on a Wednesday, they know it on the Thursday. What we do then is to alter it. Of course it makes them feel like nervous wrecks all the way through. But what a gift we have! When we go wrong we can make it look as if it's their fault.

Eric and Ernie today through the lens of Patrick Lichfield.

Ernie at school, the well-scrubbed scholar.

Eric before he needed his specs – and with much more on top. Second left, front row, at Lancaster Road Junior School in 1932.

Amazing what you can do with a straw hat. On the road in 1940.

The debonair look in 1945.

See no evil. A pensive Eric protecting the little fella – in pantomime in the mid-1950s.

With the Beatles.

With Ed Sullivan on their American début.

With Joan and Doreen, Blackpool 1952.

The Magnificent Two. Filming in the 1960s was all too different from working in television.

With Eddie Braben and Johnny Ammonds and their wives, and Doreen and Joan.

ERNIE: Somebody said it was a muscle or something up there. There are actors and actresses who learn something every night regardless of what they're working on - they'll sit down and learn something just to keep themselves in trim.

ERIC: I went home with Glenda Jackson one night and she really did learn something!

We'd like to have Elizabeth Taylor as our guest one day, but the question is, doing what? What would we do with her? Honestly, we've turned down a lot of people. It's no good just having Elizabeth Taylor without a good angle. We'd have to do a scene from *Cat on a Hot Tin Roof* or something.

ERNIE: No. It would have to be a musical number.

ERIC: Yes, perhaps, but we still have got to do something *with* her.

ERNIE: It's easy to run out of personalities. You look for the twist all the time - like when we had Arthur Lowe and Fenella Fielding in *Mutiny on the Bonty*. It was spelled wrong by accident in the script, so we decided to do it that way in the show.

ERIC: With us nothing is sacred. If it were, we would have been out of business years ago.

3

The Folks Back Home

ERNIE: You can't have a name like Eric's without associations and memories of Morecambe.

ERIC: And inevitably, Morecambe comes up in our act from time to time. I always look upon it as home. I never say, 'I'm going up to Morecambe', I say, 'I'm going home.' But my link with the place is pretty thin these days.

ERNIE: I know what you mean. My home used to be East Ardsley near Leeds. I still have many happy memories of my childhood, but with the change in lifestyles, I wouldn't want to live there now.

ERIC: For me there has been no real reason to go to Morecambe since my mother and father died. I have a couple of relatives of whom I'm very fond, but they're the only people who are still up there. What's the point of going to Morecambe and staying in a hotel? If I'm going around that area I would obviously go to see my mother's and father's graves, but I haven't been there since my mother died in May 1977. My father died the year before. It certainly wouldn't be painful to go back. I have wonderful memories of both my mother and father – I was the only child – absolutely fantastic memories, and I think of them a lot and with great happiness. I'm not the type of person who bursts into tears thinking about lost parents. When my father died, I had a little cry, and when my mother died, I had another. I haven't cried since. Only laughed, and with them, I hope – in fact, I believe.

ERNIE: I was very upset when my father died about twenty years ago. I was much closer to him than I was to the rest of the family. Even now, I can always feel a little of my father inside me. He was an amateur performer, and we used to work the clubs together. Much more important, he was a nice man, a very generous man. He didn't have much money, but he was always very generous with what little he had.

ERIC: I remember he was very ill when he was about Ernie's age. He had been a sick man for a long time.

ERNIE: Yes he was, rheumatoid arthritis and all that. My mother always said it was malnutrition. When he was a kid he came from the poorer end of Leeds and there never was enough food.

ERIC: When my father died I got in touch with Bill Cotton and said, 'My father's died; I've got to cancel the show.'

Bill thought this was wrong. He had had the sort of relationship with his father that I had with mine, which was great. He said, 'Well, I can only advise you, and it's nothing to do with me. If you want to take the time off, you go and take a week off and organize things. But I think you're wrong. Go to the funeral and come back to work immediately.'

Which I did, and it helped.

It was a good show that week. It didn't make any difference at all – not to me and I'm sure not to anyone else.

ERNIE: No, you do detach yourself.

ERIC: Up to a point. I don't think that if my wife died and I had to go on the following day, you'd get a great performance from me, but – and I know it sounds terrible – it wouldn't make any difference to a performance a week later. I'd do as well as I would on a normal show. It's the people round you who cause the problems, they spoil it by sympathy. You walk in and you think no one's going to say anything, everything's fine. But before long one of the girls is going to burst into tears. That's when it hurts. You just want to be normal at times like that, but they won't let you. And I understand why – because our families are really what it's all about. They are, as far as I'm concerned.

ERNIE: That's undoubtedly true. It's what it's all for.

ERIC: I look back to my early days and to the illnesses that I've had, all the knocks, and I still think I am the luckiest man in the world. Let's face it, doing what we do is easy – once you know how to do it. It's like drawing and painting. You just have to know how.

ERNIE: It's easy, but don't tell the others. Sure, we have nervous tension, but comparing it with the man who, for instance, slaves in a factory from, say, seven o'clock in the morning until late at night, then it really is easy. There are some people who do some very tough jobs in this world. Look at the milkman, he's up every morning at five o'clock. And the postman.

ERIC: The end result is making our families happy. We don't entertain much at home. A perfect day for us at Harpenden is when Gail and her husband Paul come down with their kids or Gary and his new wife Tracy spend some time here. The only time we really socialize is when we go to the big showbiz events and the charity balls. Then it's lovely – we meet all the pros.

Joan deals with all my fan-mail – sometimes answering thirty letters a day – occasionally working up to midnight. She deals with all the business matters, the accounts and that sort of thing. I leave the letters to her and just sign them afterwards. Of course, I feel guilty about leaving all that to her, but the practical answer is, she knows how to deal with it and I don't. It's as simple as that. I can be working in my study while she's busy with the typewriter in another part of the house.

I think Joan and I have the perfect relationship. We've gone through everything together. She's suffered over my health every bit as much as I have – and perhaps more. Together we've seen our families grow – seen Gail and Gary get married and Gail give us our first grandchild in 1978.

Actually Gail also gave us our own third child. After she gave up riding she studied nursery nursing and in 1973 brought a toddler home to Harpenden, who immediately started calling Joan 'Mum' and me 'Dad'. We took to him just as Gail did, and before long, we legally adopted him. That's Steven. He is now as much a member of the Morecambe family as are the other two.

Of course it meant more work for Joan, but she didn't seem to worry. She is everything at home – wife, mother, lover, secretary, fixer, but she doesn't get her nose into my business. I'm not at all domesticated. The only thing I was born for was sitting in a room and talking, and rehearsing and doing the shows. If the taps go wrong at home or the lights go out, she deals with it. Joan went to

24

Portugal in the spring of 1980 while I stayed behind and rehearsed. On the first night, I came home at about seven, switched on the lights and they all fused. So I went to bed at half-past seven in the dark, waiting for daylight.

Luckily, somebody came along the following day and fixed it. I didn't even know where the fuses were, although I've lived in that house for twelve years. I ought to be ashamed, but I'm not.

ERNIE: Doreen has her own toolbox, but I can do a bit more than Eric. I actually enjoy tinkering around, and I'm a good maintainer. I can do all the mechanical things, but not dish-washers or anything like that.

ERIC: I have absolutely no idea how to mend a fuse – let alone put a washer on a tap, fix the television set or mend the washing-machine if it goes. The only thing I do is show business, comedy – and fishing.

ERNIE: I can keep the motor cars going.

ERIC: I'd walk away. Soon after I got the first car I ever had I went up to the garage and said, 'Can you check the oil, please?'

The bloke said, 'Yes, sir. You need thirteen and a half pints.'

ERNIE: He said the dip-stick didn't reach the oil.

ERIC: Thirteen and a half pints and it was a fourteen-pint car. There was half a pint left.

ERNIE: It couldn't happen to me because I keep everything maintained. I can check the water and the oil. I can just about change a wheel.

ERIC: The thing I do when I get that situation is to lie down in a lay-by about four yards from the car.

Someone will soon stop. 'Are you okay?' he'll ask, and I'll say, 'I don't feel very well.' And then, between gasps, I'll say, 'Incidentally, my car's not doing very well either.'

I guarantee the chap will turn into a Good Samaritan and say, 'Oh, it's Mr Morecambe, isn't it? Okay, leave it to me.' I've done that many a time.

ERNIE: I was driving down Western Avenue once and got a puncture right in the middle of all the traffic. A guy stopped in a van and immediately said he'd help. He fixed it – changed the wheel. 'Here's a pound,' I said, but he wouldn't take the money. You try changing the wheels on a Rolls! Believe me, they weigh a ton.

ERIC: You should have given him a fiver, a pound a minute.

ERNIE: No, one pound was enough. I didn't want to spoil him.

ERIC: Despite all that, I love driving.

ERNIE: But there's nothing like having a puncture in the fast lane of the M4 while everybody around you is doing seventy and you've got to cross all the lines of traffic to get on to the hard shoulder. I can assure you the tyre's no good by the time you get across there.

ERIC: I wouldn't be either.

But I'm a lot more efficient at my work. I have two separate lives. None of my children has anything to do with show business. My elder son came into the business for about a year and couldn't take it. He works in a hotel in Cambridge now.

ERNIE: Our families come and see the show, and make comments. Sometimes they're right, sometimes wrong. They can give you reactions based on natural instincts, but then most people can do that.

ERIC: Not that they don't sometimes try to give advice. It's the 'why didn't you?' questions that I don't like – from either of our wives. I feel like saying, 'You do it', or perhaps, 'Well, why the hell don't you write it then?'

ERNIE: The questions often involve the guest stars. 'Why didn't you get so-and-so?' or 'Why did you have him?'

ERIC: 'Why did you let her wear that dress?' or 'Why didn't you tell us?' They have no idea. Neither of them, his wife or mine. Really, the only thing that I want from my wife as far as our shows are concerned is praise. I know when it's not too good, anyway. But I'd like praise all along the line, even when I know it's bad, then I know she loves me.

The thing is, our wives are not showbiz successes, as we are.

It's very easy for anyone – Joan, Doreen, or even people in the business, to come in and say, 'What's it all about? That wasn't very good.' Ernie and I *know* if a thing isn't right.

ERNIE: That's show business. You can spend £200,000 and it won't work. Build the scenery, write the lyrics, the book, the music and it seems a great idea at the time. But when you put your money where your mouth is, it becomes the old story. At least, we don't put *our* money there, we put our reputation through it and that's just as important.

ERIC: And ninety-nine times out of a hundred it works. But our wives don't know whether it's going to. When my mother said she couldn't go shopping in Morecambe after a disastrous show, I just laughed.

26

ERNIE: Our families are so close to us that they can be hypercritical if they get involved in criticism. Sometimes they make sense and sometimes they don't. I've heard people in my family say, 'Well, I was a bit disappointed about . . .' But I reserve the right to say either 'You've got a point there' or 'Don't be stupid'.

ERIC: It's back to the argument that, at the end of the show, it's up to us. If it flops, it's our fault. We get the blame, and we get the applause when it goes right. Our wives understand that it's our responsibility. We can't go on stage or before the cameras and say, 'I'm doing it this way because my wife suggested it.' I couldn't even say, 'Forgive me, but I've just broken my leg.' The audience just doesn't want to know.

ERNIE: In fact, the audience is saying to you, 'Be good tonight.' But you've got to be good *every* night because while we're always the same, they – the audiences – are always different. They've paid their hard-earned money – £3 or £5 or whatever – for one performance and they want as good a show as you can give them that night. They won't care that you were pretty good yesterday.

We work from conviction all the time we are performing. But sometimes an odd laugh here, an odd laugh there, in rehearsal or in a run-through, can mislead you terribly. Then there is a risk of playing up a line which we had no intention of making important in the first place. When it comes to the actual performance, our original judgement might well prove to be the soundest and the jokes we thought to be the best get the most laughs. That means a change of timing from the run-through.

ERIC: If four people are talking while you're doing that run-through, you think that they're not interested. We don't know that someone has just dropped dead in front of them!

I don't think the people working with us are ever yes-men, though they could be maybe-men . . . 'What did you think of it then?'

'Well, I thought it was . . .'

'Great?' I suggest.

'Um . . . yes . . . but . . .' 'Actually, I didn't think our opening was too good'.

'No, neither did I . . .'

That's what you get.

'If we had altered that, if Ernie and I had gone on and done it the other way?'

'You're right, if you could have done it like that...'

ERNIE: There have been performances after which agents and other fellows come around and say, 'That wasn't very good, was it?'

And quite truthfully, I've answered, 'No, it wasn't; I don't know what went wrong.'

Then they go on confidently, 'Well, it didn't seem to be right, did it?'

And we say, 'Well, we'll have to have a re-think about it.'

We change it for the next performance and it goes terribly well, and the same fellow comes round and says, 'I told you so.' But he hasn't told us anything. Wives can be like that, too, and my mother was just the same. But not my father; he was just happy that I was on television.

People talk about programme doctors, people who put things right in show business. But when you get a show that starts off all wrong there are very few people who could put it right. They think they can, but they can't. If its original concept is no good, you've had it. It's very rare that somebody comes in and says, 'I *don't* know the answer.'

ERIC: Very recently someone said at a script meeting, 'This is a great sketch. I will lay my bottom dollar on it, and if it isn't a success, I'll open a sweet shop.' He read it out and we laughed and we laughed; finally we were all quiet. It went down like a Stuka dive-bomber – from a high level straight into the ground. The first page and a half was hilarious and then it went lower, lower and lower. It was guaranteed by a man on whom we normally rely tremendously. But eventually, with seven or eight people at the meeting, I said, 'It's hands-up time. Who thought that was funny – that last part, in particular?'

Not a hand went up. Eventually, the chap who pushed it at first admitted he didn't think it was funny either.

ERNIE: In the final analysis *we* have to make the decision what to do. That is all that we have to do; we've got to put it over right.

ERIC: There are two ingredients. One is, making decisions and, essentially, being able to make them. The other is a great gift that somebody's given us – and I'm not a believer – is to make a line, after we've said it on perhaps ten thousand occasions, sound as if we say it only once. Obviously, we go wrong some of the time, because nobody can be perfect, but if anybody's near perfect, it's Ernie and I.

28

ERNIE: Yes, being able to speed it up at the time when it needs speeding up, and slow it down when we know we have to do so until the show starts to take off.

ERIC: We get tremendous rows – not rows, but stand-up laughing matches – with our producer Johnny Ammonds, who says, 'Don't you feel you were too slow on that routine?' We always say, 'The reason that we were slow on that routine was because the audience was slow. They didn't laugh. And you just can't go like a bullet through a routine that isn't getting laughs.' You've got to work at making it funny, visually and verbally, even after doing it for forty years. And we are professionals.

4

The Changing Faces of Comic Characters

ERNIE: Our stage appearances are probably all behind us now. We gave up pantomime because the work was too hard and stopped doing summer seasons for much the same reason. We began to spend more time at home – and we liked it. It was almost an office job. All we are really doing now is specializing and packaging. I don't think there will be any more bank raids. We did a couple of them in 1978, but people didn't realize how much we had cut back by then. I presume that if it came to the push we would do a little sequence on a charity show, but little more.

ERIC: We didn't have any big meetings to make policy decisions about this. It just came out in normal conversation.

I said, 'I don't think I should work quite as hard,' and Ernie replied, 'Of course you shouldn't.'

ERNIE: The thing is, we've both done what we need to do to stay on top. I've been ambitious all my life. I was a pusher from the beginning. It's always been push, push, push. Although we've made it now, and we don't have to try so hard, we still enjoy making personal appearances, even if it's just opening a shop. It's money for old rope, isn't it? They pay you, you go along there and socialize, what's wrong with that? The only embarrassment comes where there is no business.

ERIC: Oh, it would be terrible if there were nobody around that shop while you're getting your money, to say nothing of the lunch and all the directors around you saying, 'Oh Christ, we saw someone here last week who packed the place. Hughie Green was much better than you.'

ERNIE: It's never happened to us. But I suppose it could, if we weren't publicized right, or if they got a bad day for it. We have had the occasional small crowd, although frequently the streets are jammed. It depends where we do it. Go to the middle of Wood Green on a Wednesday and it's not going to be too good. If we went somewhere up North like Huddersfield, where we are more of a novelty, we would probably get a huge mob – particularly if the kids were home from school. The date matters, too, although I think that the day of the 'personals' is almost over.

ERIC: Funnily enough, I think the hardest medium of all is radio. I don't like it because I'm not a very good reader. I read too quickly and I sound as if I've got a plum in my mouth. And there's no money in it. So what's the point in working your cobblers off to learn a radio show script when you can do the same thing on television, be seen by millions of people and earn a hell of a lot more money?

ERNIE: When we start analysing our good fortune, a great deal of it comes from the fact that we came in at the tail-end of the music hall era, and we were young enough to start again in a new medium, television.

ERIC: If we hadn't gone through the transition, we would have ended up as unknowns doing the whole of the North in the clubs. And yet we would have been the masters of that circuit. No matter where we go we take over eventually – though it might take us a long time.

ERNIE: But we needed to have experienced the knocks, working in variety. It chipped the rough edges off us – with the most abrasive treatment of all at the Glasgow Empire. That was a tough place, all right. Very nationalistic they were. They always opened the show with kilts – Mackenzie, Reed and Dorothy and their accordions, or a cripple.

ERIC: There's nothing more guaranteed to get sympathy than a crippled man playing an accordion, especially if it's a bit too heavy for him. They loved American performers, too, but they never really went for the English.

ERNIE: If the audience were in the right frame of mind, you

couldn't go wrong. We were once there doing two spots on the bill. We did the first spot and died, then when we came to the one preceding the star, it was wonderful. We did eight to nine minutes and it was sensational! They were all getting teed up to watch Lena Horne or whoever it was at the top, Anne Shelton, Issy Bonn or Joe Loss.

ERIC: But there were top English performers who would rather have had open-heart surgery like mine – without an anaesthetic – than face Glasgow. Max Miller was too scared to go and Jimmy James used to hate it – and he was a very funny man. But I'm not sure that he could have made the transition to television.

There are about eight people who did manage the move – Benny Hill, Norman Wisdom, Harry Secombe, Norman Vaughan, Harry Worth, Ken Dodd and Ernie and I. Ken Dodd is the last music hall comic that we have – he's about the youngest of us.

ERNIE: And he's still a great stand-up in the theatre. Benny Hill is about the oldest comedian in television, and in show business for that matter, and his music hall experience has carried him through.

ERIC: The clubs are not the same thing at all. They create only one style of comedian. Little and Large are club comedians. Bernard Manning is a club comic. He has tried very hard to knock all the other comedians as a gimmick but, unfortunately for him, it hasn't worked. He will say it has, and he's a big man – he could probably eat me for lunch – but as a talent he's as funny as his last joke. To be remembered you must do situation comedy. With us the audience can say they saw Morecambe and Wise, Ken Dodd or Harry Secombe in 1949, 1950 or 1958 and that they did superb routines. Those of us who made the change did so when we were young; you need youth on your side to take all the things that come.

ERNIE: When Eric and I toured in the old days, we got £35 joint, second spot on the bill, and we paid our own fares. Real unknowns can do a club today and get £100 a night – each. They've all got cars. In our day, we had to be sure we could get the last bus home.

ERIC: I was twenty-seven when I got my first car. I knew which side our bread was buttered; I didn't want to spend too much too soon.

ERNIE: Remember the Grade gag?

'Knock knock, who's there?'

'Lew and Leslie.'

'Leslie who?'

'No wonder you don't get any work.'

You absorb everything quicker when you're young. The older pros couldn't manage the transition. To be a television star for the first time at fifty-four is virtually impossible. You've got a man battering on about your key light, ordering you to come down to a certain mark and telling you that when the music starts, 'It will come out of that box over there, but keep well back.' It would kill him. We had the time to adjust while the older star performer was too rigid in his delivery. He shouted too loud because mentally he was still performing on a stage. The whole thing was too artificial for him.

ERIC: I think most of the top comedians couldn't make the transition when television first came in simply because they couldn't remember the words. They were the age we are now – which is frightening. They were offered new scripts and new bits and pieces and they couldn't learn them.

ERNIE: They simply perfected what they did.

ERIC: Norman Evans's sketch was 'Over the Garden Wall', a little thing, but brilliant. However, you can't do that six times a year for twenty years. You've got to come on and do something else. Actually, I don't think there will be any comics left at the end of the century. There may be a few stand-up comedians, American-style.

The best comic we ever knew was Max Miller. He was great, and he would be just as great today on television as he was in the halls then. He has stood the test of time. But I would guarantee that nowadays he couldn't come out in the Paisley suit and the white hat. Those days have gone.

Situation comedies will probably be the norm in the year 2000. But they will be done by actors, not by comics. It's going to be like America here eventually. Stardom just isn't going to last as long. They're going to come out with two series and then they'll be finished. Where are Rowan and Martin today? They were the biggest thing that you've ever seen, and now where are they?

No one's even looking for new talent now. There are soccer scouts, but some of *them* have no idea. I don't know of any producer who will say, 'I think I'll go up to Birmingham and stay there three days looking at all the little clubs – not the big ones, the little places that don't get the big names. I want to find a new style, a new comic, and give him a chance.' There must be dozens who would benefit by being spotted, but no one is bothering to look. What is more, there should be a permanent show right now at four o'clock on BBC1, five o'clock on BBC2 and six o'clock on ITV every day solely for up-and-coming performers, not just comedians but dancers, musicians and singers, too. Where's the talent going to come from, if you don't have that kind of thing? The major light entertainment contribution to television in this country came from the music hall and there ain't no music hall left. The clubs are not the apprenticeship ground that the music halls were.

ERNIE: Even if they do get more money much more quickly today. They have Rolls-Royces at twenty-five just by doing the clubs.

ERIC: There are one or two people who are going to get international status. But very few. You almost never hear of Scottish or Welsh stars in England – except, of course, Max Boyce and Billy Connolly. But neither of them is a Harry Lauder or a Harry Secombe.

ERNIE: But you don't *have* to be English to succeed.

ERIC: I don't think you could have a Scottish comedian succeed today in the South.

ERNIE: They've got their own show business up there. They always have done – their Jimmy Logans and other people. And Ireland is the same, they have their own show business.

ERIC: But Terry Wogan would never have been a star if he had stayed in Ireland. There's a lesson. He indicates the need for newness in television and radio. I would say he could never have become a major star without working on television or popular radio. He wouldn't have made it on the stage. The same could apply to Eamonn Andrews, the Terry Wogan of ten years ago.

ERNIE: The attractiveness of the brogue helps. Irish voices seduce audiences – even in the working men's clubs, which are amateur. Music hall, though, was professional, and our early ambition was always to become professional. We felt that when we were with the Bryan Michie discovery shows. Our ambition was to become a real turn. They used to say, 'When your name's up in the frame, you're on your own then', because as discoveries we were only really getting sympathy applause. People would say, 'He's good, but he's only an amateur.' Once you became professional, the reactions became less kind. That is why it wasn't right for *New Faces* judges to be as tough as they were. Personally, I could never do a show like *New Faces* on television. I don't like to judge other people. I don't like to sit there like God. I have no objection to being constructive, but I don't want

34

to judge other people's talents. It's like throwing Christians to the lions. If I spot a new talent, I want to see it develop, not crucified. We need amateur shows because the business is dying on its feet without the products of those programmes.

ERIC: And producers should be made to watch them.

ERNIE: I went up to Newcastle on business not so long ago and went to a club that night.

ERIC: He does a bit of brain surgery on the side.

ERNIE: I sat down in that club and saw six acts. I came back to London with a programme on which I had marked off the acts I thought worthwhile. Johnny Ammonds was producing our show at the time and I told him, 'Look, there are four people there, all good for television.' You can get on television by recommendations from people like Eric and myself. I don't tell the acts that I've seen them. Producers must look around and see the acts in their own environment without anyone knowing – simply because auditions can kill some very good performers stone dead.

ERIC: Don't tell me there's not someone in the Manchester area who is very good at working the clubs, but nobody knows, so he still can't get a proper job in the theatre or on television.

It's true that the people who are coming up now are not very good. But they *could* be good one day – there was a day when we weren't very good either. To Arthur Askey, we are the new boys; to Ernie and me, Bernard Manning is a new boy. He's got a Rolls outside his home – and two under his chin. The newest lot of comedians seem to lack creativity. They can't make new situations. Most of them just tell Irish jokes.

ERNIE: More important, they can't benefit, as we did, from the knowledge that they had a chance to build up from the number two spot at the Moss Empires. And, having worked our way up, we knew how much had to be put into a good act.

ERIC: But we have changed – and always on our own terms.

ERNIE: In the old days, our biggest influences were Abbott and Costello. We identified ourselves with them.

ERIC: I've got records at home of Ernie and me doing very early broadcasts with Sid Field and Gerry Desmond in the 1940s, like *Youth Must Have its Fling*. Ernie and I actually *are* Abbott and Costello without the American accent . . . 'And then what happened, Morecambe?'

35

ERNIE: I used to say, 'Now listen, Morecambe, you can't get away with this.'

ERIC: I all but called him 'Chuck' and said, 'Hi'm a bad boy!'

ERNIE: We didn't think we copied them, did we?

ERIC: Oh no, we thought we were being original. We've always considered ourselves sophisticated Northerners. Even then, we thought we did high-class rubbish.

ERNIE: We started off in what we considered to be an American style, but gradually we became more and more ...

ERIC: Natural.

ERNIE: Yes, natural and English.

ERIC: There have been two formulas for us on television. The first was basically the idea that Hills and Green took to ATV. Ernie was the basic straight man.

ERNIE: Sharpie, wasn't I?

ERIC: He was the sharpie, but more of a straight man than he is now. And I was the comic, who never got the girl, never even kissed one. If I saw a girl with a big bust, my hat used to rise – and that wasn't the only thing. Now, with Eddie Braben, it is completely the reverse. Ernie meets the people, the writers, the women, and is right in the middle of everything. But he's the one who gets knocked and it is I who defend him now. That's the Eddie Braben style. He has made me more as I really am. He has made me a lot sharper and a lot more protective towards Ernie. *I* can knock him – like in a Northern family – but I wouldn't let somebody else do it.

ERNIE: He is more aggressive.

ERIC: If a girl comes in now, she is for me, whereas before my glasses used to wobble up and down, and the nose would run. Now, if a girl comes in, Ernie says, 'Hello, miss', but I'm the one on the settee with her, saying, 'Well, what are we going to have tonight?' We still do a double act. The way we perform our dialogue makes it all sound like a joke. It makes people want to say, 'And then what happened?'

What Eddie Braben did for Ernie was to make him into a person. Before, anybody could have played his part. Not now, Ernie is his own man.

ERNIE: Eddie Braben gave me a lot of that with the playwriting, the plays what I write.

ERIC: He's part of an act called Morecambe and Wise and not Eric Morecambe and That Fellow He Works With.

36

ERNIE: The great thing is to be able to do sketches in that flat without anybody having any ideas that we might be queer. We even used to share a double bed at times, but no one has ever suggested there was anything immoral in it.

ERIC: I wear very thick trousers, you see.

ERNIE: In the old days people slept together in double beds, two men, two women, without any thought of homosexuality and lesbianism and all that.

ERIC: I don't know what you're talking about.

ERNIE: And nobody thought about that either in the old days. It's just people's minds these days. I've slept with older men, younger men, and there was never any question of anything like that. Laurel and Hardy were always in a double bed.

ERIC: They accepted it from Laurel and Hardy and they accept it from Ernie and me, which is a great thing, and a great gift. I think it is because we're not offensive with it. We never say, 'Your feet are cold' or 'Can you cuddle up a bit closer?' or 'You go under the sheets and see'. No, there's nothing like that going on. And I always smoke a pipe – for the masculinity. I'll tap him on the head with it.

The hierarchy at the BBC once said, 'You can't get into bed together. You have to have two separate beds.' But we thought that would have made it worse. In fact, we've never had a single letter saying we are a couple of poufs, which is marvellous. Nobody else could do that. I don't think Little and Large could do it. I don't think Cannon and Ball could. In any case, I think we've made it our own domain now.

ERNIE: Did they have pansies and things in the old days?

ERIC: Yes, they were there in the early days, in Caesar's time. In my mother and father's time, they didn't know what being a 'pansy' was. They were ordinary working-class people, or whatever it was called in those days. My father didn't know the word 'sexual' – otherwise I might have had a few brothers by now.

ERNIE: I think they knew the word 'pansy' or 'cissy', but that's all.

ERIC: Yes, someone who walked funny and had a bit of a lisp. And a limp wrist.

ERNIE: *I* never knew about that, and I doubt my parents did either.

ERIC: My parents taught me about the birds and the bees, but I learned a bit more after a little while in the theatre. It wasn't just a question of getting to know about patter and timing – though, come to think of it, perhaps it was....

ERNIE: We have been shaped by all our experiences, not only the English ones.

ERIC: We first went over to Australia at a time when they had neither seen nor heard of us, in 1959. We only did it because the Test series was on. They were great moments – we saw a Test in Sydney and Melbourne and worked twelve weeks in each place before going on to Fiji.

ERNIE: It was also the first time we went to America – New York, San Francisco, Los Angeles and Las Vegas. I took the whole world tour on fifty feet of movie film and still had a bit left over at the end for a leader. Our shows since have been a huge success on television in Australia, New Zealand, Hong Kong and in all sorts of strange places in the Pacific.

ERIC: The marvellous thing is they have drawn us very close to the audiences there, particularly to the people in New Zealand and Australia. There was a tremendous amount of mail from there when I was ill.

ERNIE: We seem to be a gathering point for the exiles. We've heard English people out there nostalgically talk about England and Morecambe and Wise in a single sentence when they have their meetings and get-togethers. In fact, they get quite emotional about us.

ERIC: I once met an English girl walking down the street in Toronto. She actually ran after me. As she tapped me on the shoulder, I thought, hello, my luck's in – but all she did was cry. Then she told me she was from Harpenden and was feeling terribly homesick. I wasn't sure whether to be pleased or not. On second thoughts I decided it was a great compliment.

ERNIE: We seem to bring tears to all sorts of people. In Los Angeles, the wife of our Ambassador told me how excited she had been to see us on 'the tube' there.

In many countries, our shows are subtitled. In Sweden, they have to do it in two languages. We seem to do well in Germany, mainly, I suppose, from a Forces audience; I know they like us in Sweden, too. I'm told we're very big with the oil sheikhs in Bahrain. I've seen our shows in Malta and in Barbados, where I also appeared live. That was in their version of *What's My Line* with a dark lady at the end of the table who wore earrings and everything else, looking exactly like a coloured Barbara Kelly. They had to guess who I was and thought I was a vicar – so I won. I think I'd rather have lost.

ERIC: So ended your career in Barbados.

The reactions of live audiences have been the same all over the world. When we did bank raids in Britain we opened theatres again which had been closed for years. Then the big American stars followed us there.

ERNIE: We also did civic centres – at Reading and Exeter. There are a lot of civic places now, where you can get marvellous audiences. We even played Tunbridge Wells.

ERIC: They never knew, but we did.

ERNIE: But there's no real comparison with the old theatres, with their boxes, the circle and the absolutely super acoustics. They were designed for relationships between artists and audiences, and you can actually feel that contact. They were built for the sort of sound that today's entertainers, who depend on microphones, just can't understand. In those old theatres your voice could hit the back wall, and you'd hear it bounce back. That's something Eric and I appreciate. It comes with a beautiful intimacy that goes very well with the red plush and the gold.

Once at a civic centre we did our act to a full house for an hour and a half. It really was sensational. At the end of the show we said, 'Are there any questions?'

A woman at the back said, 'Yes, I've got a question!' Then she walked all the way down to the stage.

'What is it, lady?' asked Eric.

'Well,' she said, 'I just wanted to see what you looked like because I couldn't see you.'

Comedy performance is based on facial expression, not just the words, and she was just too far away. In places like the Wembley Centre audiences can't see how Eric and I react to each other. I swear I lost four pounds in that big place. You can't come on and be intimate and clever. It has to be loud and funny – and big. If you're highly successful, you're away, because they like you. But, by God, if you're not liked . . . we knew that when we did the summer seasons. They were too much like hard work. And too much dependent on landladies.

People moving into digs in Blackpool immediately ask the land-lady, 'What's good?'

And she says, 'Well, the Hippodrome's the best show. Don't go to the Empire.'

It's in that order that the business is done.

ERIC: We used to have to do landladies' nights. For all the land-ladies and their friends. If they didn't like it, you didn't do good business.

ERNIE: But if they did, you were made – even if the weather was marvellous and the sun was shining and bursting the pavements. In the first houses, you could see nothing but red from all the faces glowing. It was like a heat shimmer. And of course you got steam at Blackpool – because it rains a bit more up there. They go down to the North Pier when the rain is belting down and get soaked to the skin before they come in to the show. You could actually see the steam rising. It's no inducement to laughter, is it? And if they've had a red-hot day on the beach with the sun blazing down, they're going to be sorry they've booked for the six o'clock show. That's not good for an entertainer, either. You've got that battle with six o'clock high tea, too. It's a fact of life in Torquay that you can't get a good first house. We *never* got a good first house there.

ERIC: A boarding-house works on the basis of breakfast, lunch and high tea and, whatever their bill, it is inclusive of high tea between five and six-thirty. They don't have dinner at eight o'clock like in the hotels. We had that problem before and after we became major stars. We would get good houses in the days when we worked with Lena Horne, and the audience would be glad that Morecambe and Wise were on the bill. But if Lena Horne was ill and, say, Sandy Smith took her place, the fact that Morecambe and Wise were on the bill didn't make any difference at all to the business. The customers still stayed away and wanted their money back. That's what it's all about. But the real beauty of show business is that you don't have to be educated. You don't have to have degrees or O-levels and A-levels. You just go on there and, if you can entertain, you can make a fortune.

If audiences like the name they see on the billing when they come in, then they're laughing before you start.

ERNIE: You don't play the Wembley Conference Centre if they don't like you. Our act had taken thirty-five years to build up when we played there. We knew how to feel out an audience first. We walked on there, chatted to them and then went into the routine.

ERIC: We never used any of the stuff that we used on television.

ERNIE: Unless it was a really exceptional line.

ERIC: We've told audiences: 'In one and a half hours you're going to see thirty-five years before your very eyes.'

ERNIE: There are some lines we use in live shows that really do go back to when we started – like the fat woman routine. We start talking to the audience and then Eric says to a person supposedly in one of the front rows, 'My goodness, lady, aren't you fat! ... What a fat woman you are!'

Then I say, 'Sorry, madam, I must apologize. He was only pulling your leg.'

ERIC: 'I couldn't even lift it,' I reply.

ERNIE: And then he says, 'Oh, it's a fella.'

ERIC: Mind you, if we really saw a big fat lady, we wouldn't do it. We'd look the other way because she would make us laugh. There have been times when we'd walk out on the stage and see one in the front row – a fifteen-stone lady. So we would forget the gag and look elsewhere. But we'd have to be quick!

ERNIE: Sometimes you get a person in the front who is so bored by your show it isn't true. As he looks at you, you can feel the hate.

ERIC: All you want to do is give them all back their money.

ERNIE: You work to the audience and the audience is laughing beautifully, thoroughly enjoying it. The whole place, in fact, is rolling with laughter. But all you can think of is that misery in the front.

ERIC: Finally we whisper to each other, 'I think we've made him smile, we've got him now.' We work like ventriloquists, without moving our lips. The perfect place for me was the Hippodrome, Birmingham. A super, super variety house, a pantomime theatre.

ERNIE: It holds a lot of people in a small area and they're always quick. City stuff, you see. But in somewhere like Norwich, which also has a beautiful theatre, you would have to go that little bit slower.

ERIC: Knowing which audience is going to respond to which routine comes only with experience. Monday night first house is notorious for being the toughest. Things improve on the second house and on Tuesday and Wednesday it's all right; half-day closing is murder – the shopkeepers think they are sophisticated – and Friday second house is your first big laugh.

Even now, when doing our shows we never use 'plants' in our act. When we ask for questions people always seem happy to pose them – even if they are usually the same ones like 'Is it really a wig?' or 'Show us your short fat hairy legs!'

Then they get on to Des. 'Why don't you like Des O'Connor?' 'Have you written a play lately?'

When they get into the spirit of it, we can do twenty-five minutes based on that. We always react to movement in the audience. The famous line is, 'You're late, have trouble with the bike?' to which you might get the reply, 'If I knew you were on, I wouldn't have come at all.' It's never been done to us, though it has to other people.

But there was one celebrated night when we came on, all bright and breezy.

'Right', I said, 'are there any questions you want to ask?'

There was complete silence.

'Anything at all that you want to know about the cameras?'

Still silence.

'Can we tell you something about us – or anything?'

Finally, a fellow gets up and asks, 'Should mopeds be allowed on the motorway?' That was the question, very quiet, very serious. For years I've tried to get a funny line to follow that, but I've never found one. At the time I was quite static, I couldn't think of anything to say. But I think he got a laugh – so we got one, too.

ERNIE: A lot of our success is due to those audiences. We don't kid ourselves about that. And those audiences indicate an awful lot to the viewer – mainly that what we're doing is funny.

ERIC: It's always been that way. During the war, we did a great radio show, *Workers' Playtime*. At least, we thought it was great. It was in a factory. But our act didn't mean anything to the audience and we didn't get a laugh. My mother said it was terrible. The next time we went on, we had what we thought was a terrible script. But we got huge belly laughs, mainly because we mentioned the woman who runs the canteen and Charlie Harris, the foreman. My mother said it was a great show. It got more laughs than we'd ever had before – and that made it fine. Knowing how to react to an audience is the most important weapon a comedian has. We really only got it from our music hall experience. You laugh because the rest of the audience laughs. My mother laughed because the audience laughed. Actually I'm the biggest laugh *she* ever had.

42

ERNIE: The challenge in some instances is to go out there without a thought in your head. You've got to have the nerve to stand on stage with a blank mind. Gradually something comes out.

ERIC: I remember once saying to an audience at the Wood Green Empire, where our studios were, 'Good evening, ladies and gentlemen, welcome to the show. We want you to relax and enjoy yourselves and have a good time. If you don't laugh there's a spike that comes up out of the seat.'

Timing our routine is essential, too. We learned that lesson best of all in a television show at the Prince of Wales – for what was really a *Sunday Night at the Palladium* show. Bruce Forsyth was on the same bill. Bruce went on and slayed them – it was one of his big moments. He was down to do four minutes – it was live television – and did seven.

ERNIE: The producer said to us, 'Boys, you'll have to cut your act because there isn't time.'

So we did. We cut it and got it absolutely right, but we also spoilt it. It didn't mean much.

ERIC: When we did another *Sunday Night at the Palladium* they said, 'Four minutes, boys', and we said, 'Five', knowing we had rehearsed a seven-minute act. We went on and it worked. We did seven minutes, with a wonderful batch of laughs when we came off. They said, 'You were very naughty boys – but it was good. Can you do another?' We learned a lesson with that.

ERNIE: The lesson is, don't do as you're told. We did the extra time because we knew we were right to do it. There's nothing anyone can do once you're up there on a live show. For us, it scored. But had we failed, we would have been out for good.

ERIC: No, had it failed, we would have worked quicker and come off in four minutes. We did the pushing ourselves and, because we pushed, our careers advanced tremendously – and the audience was always with us. Strangely, I often think that television audiences are slightly frightened of Ernie and me. Sometimes we get the feeling that we inhibit them. So we have to work that bit harder. It's the professionalism that takes them aback a bit.

ERNIE: They're a bit nervous of it and they don't at first respond as warmly as we would like them to. It's a different approach in the theatre.

ERIC: When we go on there and do the warm-up, there's a

tremendous round of applause as we walk on. But in the studio they don't respond in the same way.

Sometimes I say something like: 'If that's your attitude, well ...' And they snort.

ERNIE: I think they're afraid of being singled out with the camera on them. They *are* part of the show: they are as important to that show as the performers. They react differently and better to stuff that has already been filmed. When they see these routines on the monitors it is like watching them on the box at home and they become more relaxed.

ERIC: We are helped by the sort of catch-phrases to which the audiences can respond, like: 'What do you think of it so far?'

'Rubbish!'

That came off marvellously in a sketch with Glenda Jackson. But I got into plenty of trouble with it when I was a director of Luton F.C. I used to go to the away games and, if we were losing at half-time, the crowd would stand up and shout, 'What do you think of it so far?' and the answer that came back was 'Rubbish.' They were losing 2–0. Everybody quoted it. That's just one line.

ERNIE: We came out with thousands, like 'my little fat friend'; 'you can't see the join'; 'the plays what I write'; 'Lord Ern of Peterborough'; 'Little Ern'; the business of Eric putting his hand behind the curtain as if the manager has grabbed him by the throat, and, of course, the one visual one where Eric says, 'I'm going for a quick ...' – which looks as though he's having a drink.

ERIC: That was the first one we ever did. And it caught on.

ERNIE: It's identification.

ERIC: You don't write that in a script and say, 'Ah, that's going to be a catch-phrase.'

ERNIE: Publicity helps us too. We can never complain about that.

ERIC: We must be the friendliest people the press have ever known.

ERNIE: We're not rude to them and they can always contact us. They know our numbers, even though we have our own PR man, George Bartram.

ERIC: They don't have to get in touch with secretaries at special numbers or anything like that. We had a session once at a time when there were rumours that we were going to split up. I told them, 'I'll see if Ernie and I are splitting – I'll read the paper.'

5

Who's Who

ERNIE: In the 1970s we became a regular part of British showbiz. People began asking us for interviews for the weeklies and magazines. I naturally assumed they were interested in the plays what I wrote, but in 1973 Kenneth Tynan in the *Observer* started talking about Eric's Freudian ideas and his subliminal pauses.

ERIC: They worried me, those did. I thought I ought to go back to hospital. Then they wrote about us again in the *Listener* three months later. We had our picture in *Vogue*, too. Somebody must have got the message. In 1976 we were given the Freedom of the City of London and in 1977 Lancaster University gave me an honorary degree. I was a D. Lit. There's no answer to that.

ERNIE: And we got in *Who's Who* – under the names of Bartholomew and Wiseman. Percy Thrower got in the same year. But I worried about the state of the country when Denis Healey, who was then about to become Chancellor, wrote nice things about us in the *Radio Times*. He said one of his great achievements at the Ministry of Defence was meeting Morecambe and Wise.

ERIC: We knew income tax would be going up after that. Or maybe he wanted a part in one of our shows. For the moment, we were happy with the people who came out straight away and admitted they were entertainers – like Cliff Richard.

ERNIE: With Cliff, what I remember best was the flat sketch that week.

ERIC: It was about the funniest routine we had ever done. Ernie's all dressed up in modern gear because Cliff's coming and I'm totally unconcerned, sitting there building a model aeroplane. Then Cliff comes in wearing the soberest suit you could imagine; absolutely immaculate, while Ernie's covered in tassels and everything else. We're trying to prove that Ernie's a lovely mover, both a dancer and a singer, and the only record we play is one of Cliff singing 'Living Doll', which was made twenty years ago. I kept saying, 'Turn that rubbish off, I can't stand that fellow.' I was more interested in the model aeroplane.

ERNIE: We said we wanted to do a routine with him but he refused. 'I'm sorry, fellas, I hate to tell you this, but it's a bit old-fashioned.' I said, 'I saw Gene Kelly do it!'

ERIC: Now I knew that was the wrong thing to say! As I pointed out, 'Gene Kelly, she wouldn't do a number like that! She hasn't been the same since she married Prince Rainier of Meccano.'

Cliff's a very nice boy – and will always be a very nice boy, even when he is seventy-five. He's the only one who I've met who looks younger than Cary Grant.

ERNIE: Really, he was first class. And he can act. Some can't.

ERIC: He was very good on dialogue. He knows what he's doing.

ERNIE: Of course, parody plays an enormous part in our routines. But that only works if the original is as familiar to the audience as an old sports jacket. Otherwise there's no point in doing it. That's why our version of Gene Kelly's 'Singin' in the Rain' routine turned out so beautifully. Everybody knew every sequence of it. I did the Kelly bit, dressed – or so we thought – exactly as he had appeared in his film. We had a street scene modelled on the original and Eric played the policeman.

But it was what we did with it that made it funny. Afterwards, I could see that my hat wasn't the same as his and neither was the suit. He had a closed umbrella and I was using an open one. The best bit of all was when I was doing the sideways dances, twirling the brolly, while Eric was at the back swinging his truncheon. We had a woman throw water out of a window on to him. Gene Kelly didn't have that advantage. Eric was standing under a drain-pipe that dripped all over him and he ended up sitting in a filled horse trough. I didn't even get wet. It was a miracle the water worked every time.

ERIC: It was Bill King, our own prop man – he works with us all the time on BBC and ITV – who arranged things so beautifully. He's one of the greats.

ERNIE: You work it out. I came out of the door and I'm 'Singin' in the Rain ...' The point when I went bomp, be-bomp, bomp was the cue for the music and for the shot of Eric under the drain-pipe.

ERIC: It was also the cue for the water, which worked perfectly to my disadvantage.

ERNIE: Bill could have been too slow or too quick, but he was spot-on every time. Gene Kelly actually took his hat off and stood under the drain-pipe, but it was Eric we let suffer, not me. I'm not daft.

ERIC: He was perfectly dry while I got wetter and wetter all the time. It wasn't very nice at the time, but afterwards it was great to watch it all being put together.

ERNIE: I think we proved something with that routine: the efficiency of television. We did the whole number in three hours, yet it must have cost between £20,000 and £30,000 to make – to build the set, hire the orchestra and rehearsal time. Eric and I were probably the cheapest part of it.

We did a musical number with Terry Wogan in exactly one minute forty seconds and I wouldn't like to think what the cost of that was, what with the chorus girls, studio time and the sets – to say nothing of a chandelier that cost five grand and was never used. That was just for the setting.

The era of the Hollywood musicals went out because the studios couldn't afford them. Nobody could pay for a Busby Berkeley number with fifty girls.

ERIC: Swimming or standing on fountains.

ERNIE: They did it for practically nothing in those days – for about five dollars a day, with a free lunch. And all the swimming you wanted, of course. But now, few people realize how much we rehearse, and there are some performers who don't share our enthusiasm. Rehearsals were a problem with Terry Wogan. He's such a busy man it's ridiculous.

ERIC: I also think he's anti-rehearsal. I would have liked him for another day, not for his benefit, but for ours. We wouldn't then have worried about things going wrong.

ERNIE: We kept Terry secret until he appeared before the studio audience in 1980. I just introduced him by saying, 'I've persuaded a

47

well-known disc jockey to come round and talk about the pop record I'm going to make.' I opened the door, he stood there, smiled, and everyone went bananas.

I said, 'Terry, lovely to see you,' shut the door – and the lamp fell off the wall.

The audience died. Anyway, we had to re-do it. The stage manager gave me the signal. I went to the door, opened it again, but this time Terry wasn't there. Nobody had told him what to do. Eventually it came right, but if we had left the first attempt in we would have looked a bit amateurish.

Des O'Connor is notorious in rehearsal, too. He's never on time.

ERIC: He's early for lunches, but late for rehearsals.

ERNIE: He always comes in saying, 'Oh, I'm sorry, boys, I didn't know.' We always know that if we call Des for eleven he will arrive at twelve. So we call him for ten. We know all the bad habits, who will give the lame excuses.

ERIC: Des limps in.

ERNIE: But going back to the grand routines, one I was very proud of was Cliff Richard on the battleship, a sort of mixture of 'The Fleet's In' and 'On the Town'. That was back to Gene Kelly again.

ERIC: We actually met Gene once, in 1952 when we were at the Palladium. He was out front one night, then came round by the stage door. Ernie and I were waiting to go on and suddenly we saw this great man, who was quite tiny – and I'm used to tiny men – and who looked like a tall jockey. He was wearing a long touring overcoat. When he saw us he said, 'Swell', and put his thumb up.

ERNIE: I thought he meant his thumb had swollen after catching it in the door.

Years later I saw but couldn't get near him at a Variety Club lunch. There were thousands of people there.

ERIC: All with umbrellas, hitting him.

ERNIE: He was in the middle, doing an interview, and I was on the fringe. I'd just been stuck in a lift on the nineteenth floor for twenty minutes with Bill Cotton and Marti Caine. By the time the lunch started I still wasn't at the table. But Kelly didn't mind about that; he still said, ' "Singin' in the Rain" by Morecambe and Wise was one of the funniest things I've ever seen. I enjoyed it more than seeing my own version.' Then he turned to me and said, 'Thank you, Eric.'

ERIC: Which was interesting, because I was down in Hampshire on a fishing trip. I was in a little hotel watching it all on television. When Gene said, 'Thank you, Eric', I fell off the bed. Usually it happens the other way round – I'm always called Ernie. That's the only reason they put us in *Who's Who*.

Without sounding swollen-headed, nobody could do that routine again; nobody could better Gene's 'Singin' in the Rain' and nobody could repeat our version either.

ERNIE: We hope we've laid down the original and thrown away the mould.

ERIC: The Kelly routines are the most easily recognizable. The only trouble is you can't play Gene Kelly with top hat and tails.

ERNIE: That's why we like doing the Fred and Ginger bit, too. Of course, the huge staircase is an essential part of any of those routines. What leading lady doesn't want to stand at the top of a set of stairs while a dozen or more handsome men in top hats, white ties and tails are all looking up at her and singing 'You Were Never Lovelier'? They all want to do that. They have the fantasy of wanting to walk down what we call the Cricklewood stairs. The first time we did it, we only had six chorus boys. But when they turned to the camera, you could see they were Patrick Moore, Cliff Michelmore, Michael Parkinson, Robert Dougall, Frank Bough and Eddie Waring. All of them in Fred Astaire gear.

ERIC: We wondered if Patrick Moore would be worried about having to wear a new suit for the occasion, but he put the tails and the black trousers over his old ones.

ERNIE: He's got a good tailor, hasn't he?

ERIC: He's still there, working on that suit. But Patrick's a very intelligent man, and looks it – especially if his top hat falls over his face.

ERNIE: Yes. That's what is so marvellous about him, he doesn't care that people think. We had all six singing the one word 'lovelier', but we dubbed in Patrick's voice. We were frightened he'd say it so quickly, you'd need a radio telescope to pick it up.

The magic of that number was that people immediately recognized what we were trying to do.

ERIC: The style has to be one that is instantly reminiscent.

ERNIE: It's tapping people's memory banks, which Eric and I do a lot.

ERIC: Well, I do the memory and Ernie does the banks.

49

ERNIE: We had Des O'Connor at the top of the stairs once and as he walked half-way down, he completely disappeared, vanished in the middle of the staircase while we sang and danced our way to the bottom. We had a staircase idea for Shirley Bassey, too – as a follow-up to what was one of the best routines ever on the *Morecambe and Wise Show*.

She had been made to suffer the indignity of wearing a beautiful hairdo, a gorgeously expensive gown with lots of jewellery – and a pair of nasty, black army boots, with laces. We wanted her to come back on to the show. We told her we would begin with a sketch of us in the flat trying to persuade her to return. We were going to say, 'Shirley, would you like to do a number with us?'

To which she would reply, 'What, after what you did to me in those boots?'

Next would come a flash of those boots while we said, 'Honestly, we promise you, nothing will go wrong. You're at the top of the stairs in the beautiful expensive gown and once you've come down with us, doing this wonderful routine together, you'll never look back.'

ERIC: We'd tell her, 'We'll make you into a star.'

ERNIE: 'And you'll sell the record as well. You'll have some big record sales, I promise you.'

ERIC: ''Cos *your* auntie will buy one, won't she, Ernie?'

ERNIE: We wanted her to do the elegant walk down the stairs – only to discover, when she got three feet from the bottom, that the staircase hadn't been completed and we would have to help her down the rest of the way. Shirley Bassey didn't want to do it – but Penelope Keith did. And she was wonderful.

Part of our policy has always been to bring people on to the show just as they reach their peak, and Penelope, straight from *The Good Life*, was at that time beginning her own series and very much on top. Funnily enough, her secret ambition really was to walk down that glamorous staircase with the beautiful music behind her. The Ginger Rogers bit.

ERIC: She said she would do the Cyrano de Bergerac sketch we had planned for her just so long as at the end of the show she could walk down the Hollywood staircase.

ERNIE: We agreed. She came down the stairs in all her finery; we in our top hats and tails – and then we had to help her down those stairs because they hadn't been completed. It was all hands, knees and boomps-a-daisy everywhere. We never rehearsed it, we just did it. Sometimes it's better to get a bit of realism – and hands did go everywhere! We got to the point where it was fun.

ERIC: It was the first time my glasses actually steamed up before they started cracking.

ERNIE: I said, 'I'll tell you what, we'll handle you personally ...'

ERIC: She had to put her feet on our shoulders and climb down ... her toe went into my hat ... it was all ad lib.

ERNIE: You couldn't rehearse that sort of thing. We had a similar happening with a dummy once – Eric came on with this giant doll called Oggy. He was fifteen feet high. We simply got the lines, talked about it briefly, then did it. You've got to keep that spontaneity, or you lose the comedy.

ERIC: With the dummy the answer I got was yes. With Penelope, the answer was no.

ERNIE: I wonder what happened to Oggy?

ERIC: Someone pinched him – took him home. It must have taken him a week to do it. You couldn't get him on a bus.

A typical example of how ideas get out of hand – but to our advantage – was having Angela Rippon on the show. A news-reader dancing? Ridiculous. A news-reader having a sexy pair of legs? How could she? Everyone thought she was on castors. But this was going to be our secret. And frankly we didn't think about it when we got her on the show. We didn't in any way think of her in terms of legs.

ERNIE: You could say they took us completely by surprise. We made it look like a legitimate newsflash in the middle of the show, with Angela stepping from behind her desk so that people would say, 'What's going on? Has war broken out or something?'

ERIC: Christmas – and a newsflash coming on?

ERNIE: She said, 'Denis Healey said this morning there may be trouble ahead ...' And then she started to sing, '... although there's moonlight and music and ... romance'. The desk opened in two sections and you could see that she was wearing a long dress with a slit in the middle of the skirt. Suddenly, everyone knew that Angela Rippon had legs. We had expected people to call out, 'Look – Angela Rippon's dancing', but they didn't. They saw legs. I must say, she kicks beautifully.

ERIC: Anybody who gets too close –

ERNIE: She kicks very straight and very sure.

ERIC: I think she must be the highest kicker I have ever seen.

ERNIE: Eric and I over the years can watch somebody do something and tell what's good, what's right and what's wrong. We can assess it as any dancer can assess another one. And she was good. The following year we used her on the end of a line of Tiller girls.

The problem was keeping it all a secret. We didn't want anybody to know that she was going to do the show. We tried to keep the press away. I think it was the best decision we ever made, but the fuss all happened by accident. I think the girl who did the costume must take the credit for what happened. Nobody told her we just had to see her legs, because it never struck us that the public hadn't seen them before.

We had Richard Baker as well. That was Eddie Braben's idea. Richard had a briefcase and I said, 'Is that the news in there?'

He said, 'What d'you mean?'

I pursued the point. 'Is that next week's news?' I asked. 'Don't you rehearse it then? Is it all fresh?'

We always try to get something in the show that will become the big talking-point.

ERIC: But the choice is getting smaller. Actors and actresses lead different lives from comedians. Their careers are different. They will happily do a series of thirteen plays, but they then won't do that part again. Ernie and I, on the other hand, are what we are all the time. We love straight actors and actresses so long as they really give their all doing those awful lines as in Glenda's Cleopatra: 'like the beauty what I have got'. Oh, the look on her face after she had to say that! This wonderful actress, with two awards, world renowned, dreading saying it. It's written all over her face, but say it she does, because we asked her to.

ERNIE: It's like asking an actor – the bigger the actor the more audacity we show – to say, 'To be or not to be' and then query it. We interrupt with, 'That wasn't quite right, was it?'

ERIC: We go on, pointing to the look on their faces, 'That's not allowed for a start, and put out that cigarette while you're doing it.'

ERNIE: 'And walk up and down because it's television, you know. They think you're dead if you don't move.'

ERIC: Of course, they turn round and say, 'Shakespeare didn't want it like that. It has been done this way since his day.'

ERNIE: We say, 'That's why it's so boring.'

52

A few hints on doing the old soft shoe for the Prince of Wales at a Royal Variety
Show at Windsor, 1979.

Richard Baker revealing the secrets of next week's news.

Eric and Ernie are always under pressure to do publicity gimmicks.

With Robert Morley in the mummy's tomb.

Dame Flora Robson, Sir Felix Aylmer and Sir Michael Redgrave showing how it should be done – in a play what Ernie wrote.

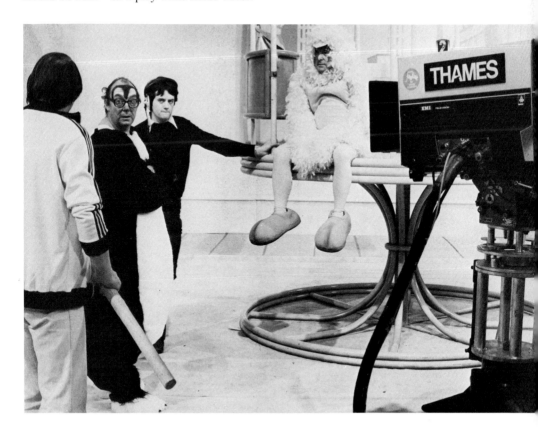

The serious side – before the cameras turn.

Ernie's contribution to a campaign he continues to support strongly.

Some useful musical tips from André Previn.

The elegant men about town, from left to right: Frank Bough, Cliff Michelmore, Eddie Waring, Patrick Moore, Robert Dougal and Michael Parkinson. Eric and Ernie were behind the camera.

Doing as the Romans did ... with the help of Glenda Jackson.

He knows how it is. Ernie with Anita Harris, Derek Nimmo, James and Susan Hunt, and Richard Burton (who later married Susan).

The big announcement: Thames Television's way of revealing their schedules for 1980 – with Eamonn Andrews, Rolf Harris, Eric Sykes, Michael Aspel, George Cole and wives.

ERIC: And Ernie says, 'Shakespeare doesn't mind it being done this way, he was contacted only this morning . . . and he's happy with Ern's treatment. Just put a hole in the tights, that always gets a laugh.'

We did that in our 1980 Christmas show with Peter Barkworth. And we got him to walk around with his finger covering the hole. There's nothing better than telling a really top actor, 'Don't raise the arm too high! It looks as though you want to leave the room.'

ERNIE: And we would use a few sound effects as well.

ERIC: But not when he's walking.

ERNIE: Actually Lord Olivier has been on the show – although I have to admit we didn't give him the full treatment. He was just seen on the telephone, one of a group of stars, all of whom we tried to persuade to come on the show. Of course none would. Larry's excuse was that we'd got a wrong number. He said his was a Chinese restaurant. 'So solly, long number.' It was over in half a minute and he didn't even film it with us. It was shot separately. It should have been better, but it was the best we could do at the time.

ERIC: The impact of having Laurence Olivier was enough.

ERNIE: We did the same thing with Yehudi Menuhin and Nureyev. Lionel Blair has never forgotten it because Nureyev said, 'What, you couldn't get Lionel Blair? You want me to do the show?' Of course, he had no idea what he was saying. Probably thought he was on Radio Three.

ERIC: It would be marvellous to get Olivier to work with us, singing 'Brush up your Shakespeare'. I'd say, 'I watched you, I saw you nearly every night in *Hamlet*. I paid 50p a seat in the gods, and you never got a laugh. Not a sound. It worked well in the end, but that's only because they know you.'

I have no respect for the great stars when they come to see us at the flat. Ernie does, because Ernie is a crawler.

ERNIE: And I get them cheap, you see.

ERIC: He cons them.

ERNIE: But don't think we're always lucky with guests. We have been known to get a thumbs-down from time to time. Michael Caine wouldn't do it when we first asked him in 1977.

'They asked me, but I had to say no,' he said at the time. He thought it would be dangerous for his career. He said he was 'not in the market' for that sort of thing and wanted to be taken seriously.

Well, we would have taken him very seriously – we might not have given him any laughs.

I went to see Sir Ralph Richardson to ask him to be in a show, but he was playing it very warily when I called at his house near Hyde Park. I had a cup of tea with him and a long chat. He didn't seem to object on principle, but what he was worried about, he said, was the writing. I think he had an idea that we do rubbish.

ERIC: True, I always say that we do high-class rubbish.

ERNIE: He said if we could get Harold Pinter to write something for him about a couple of schoolboys and a fag he would think seriously about it.

ERIC: A fag is a cigarette in Manchester.

ERNIE: I explained the whole thing to him, but when I look back on it, it must have taken a lot of nerve to ask him to be in one of 'my' plays. We didn't get much further with Sir John Gielgud, either. I asked him to appear when we met in the BBC canteen.

I said, 'Excuse me, *Mr* Gielgud' – that's what did it, I think – 'would you consider appearing in one of our shows?'

He continued eating his custard while glancing over to the far side of the room as if to say 'rescue me' to anyone who would listen.

ERIC: Ernie can do that sort of thing, I can't. I can't go up to anybody and say that. I'm tough, but I can't face being turned down.

ERNIE: Well, I always say, 'Would you consider it?' Nothing more. Some say, 'I'll consider it. No.'

Sir John knew who we were all right. He said, 'I love you boys, I think you're wonderful, but no.'

ERIC: There are people we work with now who wouldn't when we first asked them. You can't blame Gielgud and Richardson for not wanting to play Hamlet on the *Morecambe and Wise Show*. After all, they have thirty years of knighthood behind them – and they know we're going to take the comical out of them. But we did persuade Sir Alec Guinness to come on our 1980 Christmas show.

ERNIE: Even Charles Laughton, who most people would consider one of the very great actors, appeared with Abbott and Costello as Captain Kidd.

But we don't have the money for these people. That's the problem. It's more of a goodwill thing, with the difference that with us there is a little bit of love too. Sarah Miles was the only guest who was

54

booked and who didn't do the show. We sometimes wonder if she didn't show the script we sent her to Robert Bolt, her husband, who would have then told her she'd be mad to do it.

ERIC: You can't retire on the money we give, that's for sure. But then, other people have that problem.

ERNIE: Even Des O'Connor!

ERIC: I always blame Eddie Braben for the start of the Des O'Connor feud, in 1972. It was his idea. We did it first in the show when we had Pete Murray as our guest. I was a Royal Flying Corps officer in the First World War, complete with very, very big trousers. The gag was, the phone rang and Ernie said, 'I've got some great news.'

I said, 'What? Has Des O'Connor got a sore throat?'

It was the first anti-Des joke, and people laughed. He was very big at that time and it got just the sort of reaction we wanted. It was also a nice way to show our admiration. When people set out to be comedians – like Des and Max Bygraves – which is hard, solid work, and then develop the singing side much more, we do, in all honesty, envy them a little. The singing side takes off and they make an enormous amount of money with something that looks much, much easier. They seem to manage with so little effort. Here are we doing fifty jokes and one song, while they do fifty songs and one joke. That's when I wish we could go out there and be as popular as Flanagan and Allen were when they sang.

ERNIE: Yes, I think we are a little bit envious of that. And Des still looks good, doesn't he? He's still handsome.

ERIC: When we first started knocking Des I don't think his family liked it. But we had some marvellous gags about him. What makes me laugh is when people ask, 'Why don't you like Des? It's not very nice, is it?' Well, you just don't work with people you don't like, and we've worked with Des four times now on television. Des did our 1975 Christmas show, and he knew all along he was going to get knocked. We were also determined not to let him sing, however hard he tried. Mind you, he had the last laugh. He called us in the middle of one of our sketches pretending to be Alfred Hitchcock and said he wanted to see us immediately at the Savoy. By the time we got back he had – I hate to remember it now – done his song in spite of us.

ERNIE: It was during that show that he read out a list of our insults, written on a long roll of pink toilet paper. 'Des O'Connor's a self-made man,' I had said of him once.

Eric said, 'How nice of him to take the blame.'

But that's show business. There should be more of that sort of thing. Des actually rings us up if we *don't* insult him.

ERIC: He'll say, 'You haven't done the joke, you haven't mentioned me!' Personally, I always like to talk about his rise to obscurity.

He appeared on our 1979 Christmas show, when I brought on his latest record and sat on it to break it. He knew I was going to do that – because it was his idea!

ERNIE: Don't forget we knew Des from our variety days. We once followed him on at the Glasgow Empire when he had been so scared of the audience that he had faked a faint in order to be taken off. You need a terrific nerve to do that. We could only die!

People think we do put-down humour, but we don't. Of course I can say things like, 'It's a great pleasure for you to meet me', because I've got the ego of the successful playwright.

ERIC: Then Ernie goes out of the room and I say, 'Don't hurt the little fellow.'

ERNIE: Sometimes we allow the tables to be turned – just for a bit. There was the show in which Robin Day interviewed us.

'Why don't you resign?' he asked me. 'You're next to an idiot.'

'How do you do?' I answered. Then I exploded, 'I didn't come here to be insulted!'

'Oh,' he replied, 'where do you usually go?'

ERIC: Comics should be able to work together, it's as simple as that. Very few can, because they're always afraid their audiences will think the other fellow's funnier than they are.

ERNIE: They try scoring off one another, that's the trouble. The Americans are much better than us at that; they insult each other with marvellous put-down lines. Don Rickles, the greatest man in that line, insults everybody left, right and centre. British comedians resent that.

ERIC: Des has that priceless quality – enthusiasm. It makes working with him – or anyone like him – so good. The other vital ingredient is a well-known, individual image, which we can exploit to the utmost on the shows.

ERNIE: The press helps us with that.

56

ERIC: My glasses are my trademark, Bruce Forsyth's legs are his. When photographs are taken of me the only ones they're going to print are when I put the glasses on sideways. I've got more pictures with glasses on the side of my face than I have wearing them normally. I don't really know how that started. My wife tells me to take my glasses off in bed because they cause a draught. I always did things with my glasses, putting them on upside down to make friends laugh, and it caught on. I always whisper to people that I'm with, 'This is the one they're going to print.' And when you look at the papers, it is. That sort of thing used to happen in Hollywood with the big stars and we like to think that we are partly reliving that era.

When I was six years old, and Ernie seven, we used to watch George Murphy and Janet Gaynor and all those people achieving wonderful things in Hollywood at a time when the comics were really funny, and Louis B. Mayer and Sam Goldwyn were the Lew Grades of the day.

ERNIE: We thought we'd get Lew Grade on the show once. It was based on when he tried to persuade us to do a new ATV series for him.

ERIC: That was the time we walked up the stairs with our agent – who was Billy Marsh then, and still is, as far as I know – and I said to Ernie, 'You know, Lew smokes cigars like some people eat chips.'

ERNIE: I was wearing a brown hat, brown suit and brown shoes that day.

ERIC: And Lew picked him up, put his head in his mouth and lit him.

When we saw him, he'd got a nine-inch cigar in his mouth. You could perch on the end of it.

I said to Ernie, 'I've got some Manikins. We're going to offer him one of these and say: "Now put that out and have a real one."'

Well, Lew came in, making his entrance through the side door; the cigar came through first and three minutes later it was followed by him.

He said, 'Hello, boys.' He wasn't a lord then, just 'Your Majesty'.

We said, 'Hello, Lew, how nice to see you', and then added, 'Put that out! Try one of these.'

All he said was, 'I don't smoke those', and never even saw the joke. We didn't get on that day.

But there are no hard feelings between Lew and us. I was only with him the other day and I said, 'Hello, Lew, how are you?'

He said, 'Sorry, Eric, you haven't been so well.'

Very nice.

ERNIE: He also said he was sorry he didn't make a big success for us in America. 'That's the one thing I'd like to have done for you boys, to have got you away in the States.' He had promised us the big American stars when we were working with him.

'Who?' we asked.

'Peter Nero,' he said, 'one of the finest singers ...' Must have paid him in cigars.

ERIC: He sent us a big box of them for a present. I think they're worth a fiver each – twenty-five in a box.

ERNIE: He smokes ten a day.

ERIC: It was very nice of him to do that, but it made no difference of course.

ERNIE: The routine we built on that one was to have Eric come on smoking. I said, 'I didn't know you smoked cigars! How much do they cost?'

ERIC: '£2 each.'

ERNIE: 'How many do you smoke?'

ERIC: 'Ten a day.'

ERNIE: 'That's £20 a day, £140 a week. How much is that a year?'

ERIC: 'That's a hell of a lot – £7,280 a year.'

ERNIE: 'You see that little café across the road? That nice little café where everybody nips in? It's always very, very busy. If you didn't smoke cigars you could own that.'

ERIC: 'Do you smoke cigars?'

ERNIE: 'No.'

ERIC: 'Do you own that café?'

ERNIE: 'No, I don't.'

ERIC: 'Well, I do.'

ERNIE: People say Lew's cigar smoke is the ring of confidence.

ERIC: We also wanted to use Lew on the show as a Charleston dancer – he used to be a champion. Bernard Delfont was the agent for Lew then.

ERNIE: He did it on an American spectacular. We had an idea at the time in which you would just see the cigar while he stood in the wings in silhouette. It was like in the old Hitchcock television series. When you think about it, Lew Grade could open his films with that image, couldn't he?

58

ERIC: He seemed very interested. In fact we got a definite maybe. Which is no.

ERNIE: He would say, 'I'd love to, but I can't, I really can't.'

ERIC: You don't hate them for that.

ERNIE: You have to think of everything. That's what our business is all about.

ERIC: I had an idea about using Frank Sinatra on the show. Of course you would never actually see him.

ERNIE: The camera would follow us to the side of the stage.

ERIC: And we'd introduce him saying, 'Ladies and gentlemen, we've had some great stars on our show, but tonight we've got the big one: Frank Sinatra.' The spot would come up and follow us into the wings as we're watching and talking.

ERNIE: Then you'd hear him sing.

ERIC: The camera stays in the wings all the time. Naturally, we'd be the ones off-stage saying, 'Isn't he wonderful?' and 'Aren't the public going to enjoy this?' Then we could be seen to be having a fight with him behind the curtain.

We wanted Raquel Welch. I don't suppose she would have said no, but her manager told her, 'You do it separately, you don't do it with those two fellows.' So that was the end of that.

ERNIE: Tom Jones was on one of the shows. We had worked with him in New York at the time we were doing an Ed Sullivan broadcast. He came to us for a bit of advice. We told him, 'Just go on and do your two minutes and come off.' We said the same to the Beatles.

ERIC: They asked us, 'We're going to America in a few weeks, have you got any advice to give us?'

'Well,' we warned them, 'you won't be as big over there as you are over here.'

ERNIE: We said, 'They won't notice you, just go on and do a couple of minutes and leave.'

But when Tom Jones worked with us on our show in 1971 he did a very good number, very effective – 'Exactly Like You', which had been an Andy Williams record. We danced at the back, but we could never really get near to him. I loved the suits he wore – he looked like Mighty Mouse.

ERIC: He had more managers than there were people in the audience.

ERNIE: And we couldn't get a picture with him, either.

ERIC: I don't think he knew about it. The gang around him wouldn't let us have a picture taken. We had one taken with nearly all the stars – but not him. I have a collection of them at home.

ERNIE: Jones's men controlled the pictures and were frightened they might get into American magazines without his being paid for them. It's terrible talking to people like that through third and fourth parties. All you get are messages like, 'Yes, he'll be there at four o'clock.' Getting them to rehearsals is nearly impossible. We really feel like the hired help sometimes – chasing them around and doing the best for them. Of course, it's doing us good as well, but they are the big star and we're kept in our place. Tom Jones may be Welsh, but he was caught up in the American syndrome. I must say I'd like, though, to get Larry Hagman – J.R. – to appear as one of our guests.

ERIC: I wouldn't. Most of the Americans I've worked with – and I won't mention any names – I found very difficult. First of all, they don't really understand Ernie and me as comedians. They don't know our work – we're foreign to them and they're foreign to us. Nine times out of ten an American will be using a chance to go on our show as a working holiday, so getting them to rehearse is difficult. We are believers in rehearsals and I don't want the fear of them Donald Ducking it up for us....

ERNIE: Jack Jones was a typical example.

We said to him: 'Jack, we're going to rehearse on Sunday.'

'Oh,' he replied, 'I was planning to have my Sunday dinner.'

He wasn't very happy. We had him singing on the show, with just a little bit of dialogue.

When Peter Nero did appear, Eric was on the piano, Sid Green was on bass and Dick Hills on drums. I was talking to him about this great piano act that we've got, but all the time he insisted on using cue cards. Cards are not easy for me because if my eye catches one I'm liable to lose track of what I'm thinking about. Half-way through he mouthed at me, 'They've flipped the wrong card and I don't know what comes next.'

There was a hoo-ha over the dialogue for about three or four minutes. We got back to our places, but I think I aged ten years in those minutes. It was all live.

ERIC: Well, one of us was. I remember walking over three bodies.

ERNIE: Just occasionally, we imagine inviting on to our show a star whom we know would be difficult to get. Discussions go like this:

'I'll tell you who we could get! He's a big star and hasn't done much work recently. Offer him twenty-five thousand.'

The star is contacted but says, 'What! I wouldn't consider working for less than fifty.'

To which we reply, 'Give him fifty.'

So we've got him.

ERIC: Talking in dollars, of course.

ERNIE: Oh yes, I'm talking dollars.

ERIC: But thinking in yen.

ERNIE: What you don't tell them is that it's really Thailand tickles. Mind you, we wouldn't be too happy working for anyone else, either. We don't like to be guests on someone else's show. We insist on controlling our own careers, and we'd rather do that on our own show.

6

For Love and Money

ERIC: There's no question about it. What we do, we do for the money it brings us – though we've never stopped enjoying our work.

ERNIE: I like the goodies.

ERIC: That's what we work for, we work for the money to have the goodies. People say we should be at the stage where it becomes irrelevant. But you're never at that stage. Paul Getty never got to it. While you can work, you'll work and earn. Probably, there will come a time when we stop working and then we'll stop earning. But by then we hope we will have done enough with our money and saved enough, too.

ERNIE: With taxation as it stands today we can live well, though we can never really accumulate. But we *like* working – don't let anyone forget that. We've got show business in us. We're hams.

ERIC: Funnily enough, when we're working, we never think of it in terms of money. We are much more likely to worry whether an audience is enjoying the show – and if we are not getting through to them, why?

But we are galloping with inflation like everyone else. If we want a bottle of champagne for the dressing-room it can cost us £30. So we try to get it written into the contract. Ernie always reads through the contracts anyway. I try to, too, although I get lost when it comes to the bit about the party of the first part.

ERNIE: He's going to the first party while I'm off to the second party. I try to work them out for ourselves because our experiences with contracts drawn up by other people haven't been good. Today, we try to gets drinks for entertainment written into the contract. They come under 'Sundries' . . . Would you care for a glass of sundry?

ERIC: Like an orange juice.

ERNIE: Nor should it be forgotten that we have to give tips to the staff.

ERIC: He gives them the winner of the 3.30.

ERNIE: At one time we used to give presents to people on the show.

ERIC: Now what we say is, 'Let's throw a party – let's all go out to a Chinese restaurant.' We get the bill, that's all. People enjoy that.

ERNIE: In the old days, it was a traditional thing in pantomime to give presents at the end of the show – everyone did that. If you got one you didn't like, you took the name off and gave it to someone else. But not now.

ERIC: We used to throw last-night parties.

ERNIE: Yes, there was always a last-night party. That was in the last week. But it's all disappeared. People got out of the habit.

ERIC: Thames throws a little party for us at the end of a series, but at the BBC we did them ourselves. After every show we would invite people round to our dressing-rooms for a quick drink.

ERNIE: It was champagne in paper cups, wasn't it?

ERIC: Oh yes, keeping it cold in the bath.

ERNIE: But the days of free spending have really gone. That's why we still see our business as a means of making money. And why we've done commercials.

We did one for Tennent which was only shown in Scotland and in Northern Ireland. We also did them for Texaco and for W.H. Smith, and one for Dulux paints.

ERIC: But there were problems. At that time we had a contract with the BBC which said we couldn't do a commercial while making a series for them. Finally we came up with a solution. The commercial only showed our legs. Our voices were there but two faceless men were supposed to be Ernie and me. We were just voice-overs. There was nothing about voice-overs in the contract. Interesting, isn't it? The BBC realized they weren't dealing with mugs.

ERNIE: If somebody asks us to plug some toothpaste, we immediately ask: 'Where?'

63

If it's on television we tell them, 'That's expensive – because we're big on television. But what about the newspapers? What about the hoardings?'

Often, they'll settle for the hoardings. When Tennent wanted us to plug their lager we had to confine it to Scotland and Northern Ireland, because we were already advertising Watney's in England. We couldn't do two different beers any more than we could do two different toothpastes. They were decisions we made ourselves, not on our agent's advice, as a lot of people think. Our agent puts it into working order. But with contract negotiations and things like that, we now go through all the small print ourselves. We don't want to have to rely on a lawyer. If we did, we would never do anything.

ERIC: Commercials are fair game. We've often considered parodying them, but in most cases that would just be cheating. Pantomimes are full of nothing but commercials these days. Mention Brillo pads and everybody falls about laughing. To be good they have to be very clever. Eddie wrote a marvellous quickie for our 1980 Thames series. It showed me serenely smoking a pipe. There was no mention of a brand of tobacco. I said that I smoked it because it was cool, fragrant and extremely cheap. It was called 'His' – and the camera came round just as I handed Ernie my pipe to fill.

We'd like to get a midget – or Ernie dressed up as the kid – in one of the Fairy Liquid adverts with me as the woman. We'd do the advert straight and then hit the kid over the head with a frying-pan.

ERNIE: There's one thing that we want to do very much. It's a natural, but we haven't got round to it yet. The Hovis one.

ERIC: We would use exactly the same location as on the commercial with Ernie walking up the road as the little runaway boy. I'm the postman, and he's having his sandwich as I say, 'Where are you going?'

'I'm going to London,' he tells me.

'Oh lovely,' I answer. 'Post these letters for me, will you?'

ERNIE: Although we do commercials we don't go much for status symbols, Eric and I. Somehow they have never really mattered. They have never been near the top in our priorities – except, I suppose, our Rolls-Royces. They are our 'I'm-doing-well' cars. I don't really need a Rolls-Royce and I'm perfectly happy with a smaller car. But it is a question of image, of facing garage attendants who will say, 'I thought you'd have a Rolls!' And then if you go regularly to a garage in it and suddenly appear in a smaller car, they wonder why. 'Have you sold it?' they'll ask, suggesting all the time that I couldn't afford it any more. So we have them so that people won't think we're on the skids.

ERIC: I hardly use mine.

ERNIE: People like to see us in them. There's none of the usual jealousy you often notice in poorer districts when a Rolls-Royce drives by. Strange, isn't it? It's as if they are thinking, Ah well, you worked for yours, you deserve it. People still expect it of stars, although the age of the star is quickly disappearing.

ERIC: Yes, there may be fewer and fewer stars, but they will earn so much more – money, I'm talking about.

ERNIE: But back to status symbols, we have them in the same way that some stars go in for expensive clothes. We don't bother dressing smartly half the time. We just wear slacks. I remember someone once said to Paulette Goddard, 'If you're a real star, even when you put the trash out, you must do it immaculately.'

ERIC: Her husband, Charlie Chaplin, said it.

ERNIE: You're supposed to be a star all the time. With us, a suit after a while becomes a uniform.

ERIC: The mail comes in in the morning and I look at all the invitations. I say to Joan, 'Check up and see if it's dress suit.' When it is, that's the working suit as far as I'm concerned. It's the same with jewellery. Look at the watches we wear. Just a couple of cheap ones – £25, this one cost. It's stopped, but it's still right twice a day.

ERNIE: You lose sight of these things now. And yet when we were kids, nineteen or twenty or so, the chance of a decent suit was our life's ambition. You had one of those great suits that was specially made and you were the bee's knees. You were made. You had it copied from some great film star and as you walked down the street you *were* that star.

ERIC: I wore my father's suits for years.

ERNIE: I wore a suit from Dickie Henderson Jnr. I may not need the amount of suits I have now, but I like having them.

ERIC: I don't swim, yet I've got a pool here and abroad.

ERNIE: I like to swim and I like a pool. But it is a luxury.

ERIC: My kids love it.

ERNIE: I call mine an intensive care unit. I'd love an indoor one if I could afford it.

ERIC: So would I. We don't brag about our pools, but they are as much a status symbol as having a home backing on to a golf course. Mine backs on to a golf course and Ernie's backs on to a river. We both like quiet comfortable houses with lots of outdoor space.

ERNIE: But calling my pool an intensive care unit was no joke. I swim to try to keep in reasonable health. I had a tennis court built for the same reason, and that is why I have a sauna. It's simply there to keep me fit to do my job.

ERIC: I suppose if I could swim, I'd look upon it differently. But I can't. I'm petrified of the idea. I'd rather go and stand in the river and fish. Or look at the fountain in our fishpond. It's safer.

ERNIE: That's a dangerous mistake. If you toppled in, you might never get up.

ERIC: But if you drown, it's supposed to be the best death possible. You see all your life rushing in front of you. It happened to me once and I liked it so much I ran back and did it again. Actually, I nearly drowned as a kid. That's why I've never been in deep water since. My wife tries like hell to get me to watch a swimming programme. She says, 'There's a fifty-year-old man there learning how to swim.'

I say, 'Well, he's younger than I am.'

ERNIE: If you did start swimming in your pool, likely as not some photographer would come and take pictures and print them in the papers.

ERIC: What always puzzles me about British reporters and newspapers – I don't know whether it happens in America too – is the way they try to put price tags on everything, even with sportsmen. You get something like 'Liam Brady, who played for Arsenal, stepped out of his £14,000 car into his £14 pair of boots and fastened his £7-a-pair boot-laces around his £2½-million legs' or 'Eric Morcambe walked out of his £25,000 swimming-pool into his £47,000 Rolls-Royce and went off using petrol that cost £1.50 per gallon'.

ERNIE: 'And ate a couple of 14p Mars Bars.'

But having the money to spend on these status symbols is the important thing. They often say that people from the poorest backgrounds do best simply because they did have to pull themselves up by their boot-straps. Money means security to me. The more money I have, the more security I have. One fellow said to me, 'I wouldn't have thought you'd have been worried about money, I'd have thought you'd have leather-bound books or something like that'. I've often wondered about that – how would I feel if I didn't have money again after all those years?

ERIC: You've got to have the ambition to get it, and that is why we don't relax. All my heart trouble was due to the tension, the pressures and the adrenalin. I'm one of those people who feel tense all the time. It's hard to relax.

ERNIE: A perfect example of that comes when we rehearse. If we were doing a sketch with our producer or choreographer, say, we would rehearse it at a perfectly normal, comfortable pace. But put six strangers in the room and you wouldn't recognize that sketch. We would perform, conscious of their reactions, straight away. To this day, we record everything we do in the studio. We don't like to stop. Unfortunately, things sometimes go wrong, technically. But we like to do it in one go without stopping. That's the old variety trick.

ERIC: We know it's a recording, but it's live as far as we're concerned.

ERNIE: Even so, Eric couldn't relax. He looks relaxed, but he isn't.

ERIC: I don't know why. That's part of my problem. I don't think I should ever have come into show business, you see. I'm an enigma, a one-off. I should have done what my father did – been a labourer. Then I'd be fit now, with big muscles. I'd have thought: I'm fifty-four, I've only got another eleven years to go and then I'll retire.

ERNIE: Our business is a tension business, no matter who you are. As soon as you start, your eyes get that little bit wider.

ERIC: Sometimes I worry because I'm not worried, though I'm never nervous. My heart isn't thumping away or whatever, I'm just uptight. I usually get over it the next day, depending on how it's gone. If it's all gone very well, it's easier. If I'm not too happy with it, then it's harder.

ERNIE: I get aches and pains. My back aches and my legs ache. I feel like I've been boxing, like I've done fifteen rounds. Which in a way is what I have been doing – physically pulling my muscles, which have all but seized up.

ERIC: And you stretch your brain, too. You feel drained.

ERNIE: But money doesn't help that. It represents only creature comforts.

ERIC: It's building that wall around you. I put my cash into property – Harpenden and my house in Portugal. I've had it for fifteen years and only been there seven times. I couldn't find the place once after flying there – forgot the address.

ERNIE: He doesn't like the sun and sunbathing.

ERIC: It isn't that. It's always worked out that I can only go away for two weeks at a time and that's not really long enough. I don't want to live there, but I'm hoping that eventually I'll be able to go for longer stays now all my heart problems have been sorted out. I would like to spend three or four weeks at a time there. That's what I say – but I know I'd get restless. I didn't go to the house after the operation. I went to Barbados instead and stayed in a hotel. Very nice, but very humid. It was the wrong time of the year, as people were very willing to tell me – afterwards. They seemed as happy to tell me that as to discuss the next television success.

ERNIE: Show people often compare notes with each other, but we don't talk money.

ERIC: I don't talk money anyway. I was out with Max Bygraves the other night and he said, 'You ought to do so-and-so because there's a lot of money in it.' I didn't ask how much and he probably wouldn't have told me had I asked.

ERNIE: No, but of course we talk shop. It's like the classic gag about the double act who split up years before and suddenly meet again in Charing Cross Road at the Express Dairy, which was the haunt of all the pros in the old days. One of them said to the other:

'How are you doing these days?'

His former partner replied, 'Well, as a matter of fact, I'm not doing badly at all. I've just done a season at Las Vegas. I was there for twenty weeks and the place was absolutely packed out and I made a million dollars.'

The other fellow said, 'I didn't hear about that.'

But his partner went on, 'And I'm doing this film at the moment and it's going to be a big one, and I've made two million dollars.'

'I didn't hear about that.'

'I've also just cut a record from which I'll get a golden disc. It's sold thousands.'

'I didn't hear about that.'

'And last week I was at the Talk of the Town and, oh boy, did I die! The audience actually booed me.'

To which the other fellow said, 'Oh, yes, I heard about *that*.'

68

A typical double-act situation.

There's another story about the comic who says when you meet him:

'I'm doing great, I was at the Manchester Hippodrome three weeks ago and I had a fantastic reception. I had to take curtain calls – about eight of them – and the audience loved every minute of it. The following week I went to the Leeds Empire and there were six curtain calls. Then I went to Blackpool, the Palace. You know that audience? ... Just a minute, weren't you on that bill?'

And you say, 'Yes.'

'Boy – weren't *they* tough?'

It is nice to have friends in the same business, but it is hard if they have not done as well as we have been lucky enough to do.

ERIC: It all depends on how often you see them.

ERNIE: It also depends on what their nature is. If they suffer from a jealous nature, it is very difficult. But a pro always knows his place, and that is an interesting point. In the days when we were on a variety bill, the top star of the show was always treated with special respect. He had to have the number one dressing-room. When you did the band call, normally you would line up all the band parts and take your turn. But not the star. He would come in and say, 'I'm sorry about this, but I'm in a hurry. I've got a luncheon', and then jump the queue in front of everybody else and do his music. You accepted that. We still treat the big names with the same respect. We agree in our simple way that they're bigger than we are. We accept that fact.

ERIC: But you don't have to be big time about it. Some people are always playing big time; we wouldn't.

ERNIE: But it would be hypocritical not to, say, use our Rolls-Royces when visiting other lesser-known performers.

ERIC: I'd send our Rolls to their house to bring them to mine.

ERNIE: The thing you have to accept with an equal in show business is that you're always in competition with them, however hard you try to avoid it.

ERIC: But we're lucky to have to worry about that sort of problem! And there are others that I have to say I'm grateful to have – like never going anywhere unrecognized. Wherever we are, we're always joined by somebody. We couldn't go to a restaurant, or particularly to a pub, and just sit there in a corner, Ernie and I. It would be easier to sit on a bus – because people wouldn't expect to see us on it. They might say, 'Doesn't he look like . . .?' But they couldn't be positive, and then they would drop the notion because it seems so improbable. Mind you, they would know if it were Ernie on that bus – because he would be arguing about the fare.

ERNIE: I moved some chairs and things into a furniture van once and people who saw me couldn't believe it. I never bother to get in touch with Pickfords or any of the moving firms when I have a job like that to do. I simply hire a van and do it myself. I can't be bothered with all the fuss of booking a firm. So Doreen gives me a hand, helps me up the back and on the stuff goes. Then I take it wherever it's going. It's cheaper that way.

ERIC: Actually, he charges more than Pickfords does.

ERNIE: I stopped at a garage on this occasion and the man on the forecourt said, 'Mr Wise, why are you doing this? Why aren't you on the television?' He couldn't believe it, and thought I'd hit hard times.

ERIC: 'It's my second job,' he said.

But you do get some of the good things in life from being well known, too. Like knowing that if I happened to break down in the car, other motorists would be around in no time to give me a hand.

People are incredibly kind. You don't have to be a pretty girl to get looked after. But being a handsome fella like me helps.

Actually, I am resigned to not being able to go to restaurants any more, although not in Harpenden. There's no problem there. But I can't walk about St Albans or Luton.

ERNIE: I go to the local paper shop without a problem.

ERIC: I do too, but I know I'm going to get stopped and pestered, especially in Luton about the football.

ERNIE: I'll tell you what is nice abroad – meet an English person and they'll say hello or something very pleasant and personal. But someone from overseas, perhaps an Indian, will give us huge big grins. They really are more star-orientated. Sometimes we get people coming up to us and saying, 'Mr Morecambe, you're my greatest fan', or 'Oh I must say, I'm your favourite'.

ERIC: They say, 'You're Morecambe', and I say, 'No, I'm not, you are.' I'm never rude. Of course, we can make mistakes and sometimes we've upset people who ask for autographs and things. When that happens, I act myself out of it. I've got to say, 'Well, I'll sign it with pleasure', even if the last thing I want to do is stay and talk. Then I just say, 'Thanks for asking', and walk away.

ERNIE: I had that once – not being very quick when someone came up and said:

'Oh, Mr Wise, could I have ... ?'

I remember saying, 'What? what?' in a somewhat preoccupied way.

And the man going away muttering, 'Oh well, if you're going to be like that.'

I felt bad about that.

ERIC: They'll never want you again. Usually, though, they are very understanding.

ERNIE: They'll make remarks like 'I won't watch you again if you don't sign my book' or 'I know you must be very busy', when you're standing about doing nothing.

ERIC: My one escape from all that is fishing. I know it sounds terrible, but that's why I go fishing at exclusive places: I know I won't be pestered. I can happily spend a week on the Test in Hampshire waiting for the fish to bite from dawn to dusk. It's wonderful, it gives me a serenity I can't feel anywhere else, and I do like to keep that private. If I go to a river where there's a load of kids or members of an angling club, all of a sudden I'm joined.

'Hello,' they say, 'have you caught many?' There's a certain look they give me when they discover who I am. 'Oh, you don't want to use it like that! Here, give me the rod.'

It's like an Al Reid sketch. I don't want to do it their way, but I've got to let them have a go at me.

ERNIE: The hardest thing is what we call the twenty questions. When we're invited somewhere – to a dinner or something – we finish up with a cross-examination.

ERIC: Whether it's at a private party or a pub people will join us in the end. They say, 'What you gonna have?'

'No, honestly ...' I say.

But they persist. 'You've *got* to have one.'

If you go on and on with your 'Honestly, I don't want anything', they go away a big huffed.

ERNIE: You're sitting there, with everybody round you, and the questions start.

'What was Glenda Jackson really like?'

'What was it like working with Angela Rippon?'

ERIC: 'What about Little and Large then?'

'I understand you don't mix socially ...?'

It can become a bit Eddie Waring.

ERNIE: Sometimes they say, 'I laughed when I saw ...' and it shows their interest. Usually you find yourself saying the same thing over and over again.

'Does Ernie really wear a wig?'

They want to see the join in my wig; they really don't believe I don't wear one, and I can see them searching for it with their eyes. Sometimes I tell them the story my barber told me. He heard another man declaring very loudly that I had a wig, and that he should know because he was my hairdresser! I'd never even heard of the chap.

'What about Luton then?' is a popular one.

But we both know that the real worry will come when they stop asking those twenty questions and are no longer interested in looking.

7

It's All in the Game

ERIC: We first moved to Harpenden about eighteen years ago. Before that we had a flat in North Finchley. There were just four of us then, Joan and I and our daughter Gail – she was six – and Gary, who was three. The flat was pretty small. One day an old man came to repair something in the kitchen, and he said this was his last job and he was retiring to Harpenden at the end of the week. We had never heard of the place, but since we were looking for a house ourselves we went down to look at it. The following week we bought a house there. We thought it was wonderful. We moved to our present home about twelve years ago. The house had been allowed to run to seed, and we spent a lot of time with builders getting it how we wanted. We extended the place a bit, made a bigger sitting-room, and created a terrace to sit out on in the summer. We're very lucky that the view from the house is all green belt, so it's unlikely to be built over.

ERNIE: I move more often than Eric does. They always think of me as from Peterborough, but in fact that's Doreen's home town.

ERIC: I like to mention Harpenden in the same way that I always mention Luton. If Ernie writes a gag in a script about Chelsea, I usually say, 'Don't talk about Chelsea. Do it about Luton.' Everyone knows I'm connected with Luton, and everyone knows I come from Morecambe. They'll never find out my real name's Blackpool!

ERNIE: We thought of calling ourselves Morecambe and Leeds

once, but we sounded like a cheap day return. It was Eddie Braben who introduced the Lord Ern of Peterborough bit. We went from Peterborough to Sudbury Court Road, Wembley, and from there to Harrow.

Now Doreen and I have a lovely house at Maidenhead with the Thames at the bottom of the garden. We keep our boat, the *Lady Doreen*, there and frequently take her up and down the river. It's one of my favourite pastimes. We always say our house is like a railway carriage because it's long and narrow, but this does mean that all the windows look out over the garden. We've also got a tiny mews house in London, but our real luxury is the new place we've just bought in Florida. I like to go there if I can make the time. Normally, when I'm not working, Doreen and I lead as ordinary a life as we can manage. We have our dog, Charlie, our garden, the boat ... sometimes I go shopping with Doreen and I read quite a bit – showbiz biographies mostly.

ERIC: Ernie travels much more than I do, but a typical gag would be me pointing at Ernie and saying, 'You're a man of the world. You've been around Peterborough, haven't you?' People begin to take in where we come from because we do it so often. It's a nice name, a good name, Harpenden. We did a lot with the Harpenden Male Voice Choir.

Through Harpenden I became involved with football. It started in 1969, about a year after my first heart attack. Gary was about ten years old when he announced he'd never seen a real football match. He'd only watched the game on television. Luton and Watford were our nearest teams, and at the time they were both in the Third Division. I suggested he decide for himself: 'Make up your mind, which team do you want to see – Luton or Watford?'

He said Luton was closer.

So I rang up Luton and said, 'Can my son and I come along to a match?'

They said, 'Certainly.' They had a new chairman, Tony Hunt, who was very good for that club. He put a lot of money into it. Later on he asked me if I would become a director and I said, 'No way. I get all the perks I want as it is.' But eventually he talked me into it.

I became a director of the club in 1970 and stayed until 1977. Working for the Town really was work. That was why I left. It was

74

getting too much into my life. We were arranging the television shows around Luton Town's matches. While I was a director I don't think we ever did a show on a Saturday. It was always a case of finishing rehearsals on Friday and doing the show mid-week. It got a bit heavy. No director picks up any money in the football game, the only thing you do is put money in – although I didn't do that at the beginning. To join Luton now probably means putting £25,000 down. You get shares, but there are never any dividends to go with them.

ERNIE: Peterborough Football Club are looking for a £50,000 loan, interest free, and I said I'll help them to find one.

ERIC: The way men make money from the game is through inviting certain people to sit in the best seats and talk business while a game is on. But I couldn't do that because there's nobody in football in show business. Having me was a tremendous PR asset. I gave Luton more publicity than they had had in the whole time the club had been in existence. I told them that if the BBC ever stopped me saying Luton on the show, the BBC would have to get someone else. I also put a lot of money into the club through opening shops, and through writing articles for papers, the cheques for which went straight to the Town. I never saw the money they earned – and I am talking in terms of £10,000 or so – and I didn't take it out with me when I left, either. I would still do the same now – even though I'm no longer a director.

ERNIE: Why Luton? Why not Arsenal?

ERIC: Because the first four letters are right. And it's closer.

The Luton directorship got me accepted as a comedy 'expert' on sport. The *Daily Express* asked if I would write an article every now and again in the paper and we started off with a series of about twenty-five. I talked to Norman Giller, usually calling him 'Sunshine' – and we did some for *Tit Bits*, too.

More often than not, Norman would just ring up and say, 'I haven't been able to get in touch, I've written the article, is it all right?'

And I would say yes. I sometimes didn't talk to him in detail. I'm not a sports guru, but I know who won the cup in 1950, because I was doing it as a gag – Arsenal. I've written about boxing and motor racing. I once went round Silverstone with Jackie Stewart at 125 miles an hour. No car, just running. That was about four years ago.

Actually, it frightened me to death, I must be honest with you. There's no fun there – not for me.

In my youth I would have liked to have been a professional footballer. Purely and simply because it meant £5 a week. That was a lot of money. My father was getting thirty bob. Five pounds a week for playing a game of football I thought was easy. But I was never ever big or strong enough to be a footballer. I suppose if I had done it, I would probably now have a little pub somewhere, or a small newspaper shop. That was the ambition in those days for a working-class lad – to be able to run a pub where the fighters, the big boxers, go.

ERNIE: My father worked on the railway and I was supposed to join him – become first a fireman and then a driver. The driver was the really top job – £10 a week I think.

ERIC: You sure they got as much as that?

ERNIE: That's the figure that I remember. My dad used to get £2 a week. He was a signal lampman and then became the foreman, but a driver started off as a fireman and the driver was the tops.

When we first went into show business, we could earn more in a weekend than my father earned for months on the railway.

ERIC: That still goes on up North. Up North people work during the day and do bits and pieces in the evening.

ERNIE: There's no doubt about it – the reason we came into show business was because we didn't like hard work. Now it is hard work, but it wasn't in those early days. Then, you could go to a club and pick up £2. My dad had worked all week for that. So it was very easy money. That's why I appreciate what I can now afford.

I like flying best, although I can't pilot a plane myself. It became the thing to learn to fly, so I had a couple of lessons and I'd like to follow that up one day. I enjoyed them because I could do it. But I gave up because I thought I'd kill myself; I thought the aeroplane would pack it in or something. It's not difficult, but it's not worth the risk either. It's the landing that's a bit tricky.

ERIC: Gliding must be a nice feeling, though I've never done it. Cricket is more my line. I'd like to have a bat and be all padded up and everything and then face somebody like Lillee or Thompson for a couple of overs to see what it really is like.

ERNIE: I like handball sport. Although I'm a dancer, I was never very good at football or anything and never any good at boxing.

Catching a ball, that's what I can do – or at least I could before my eyesight went.

ERIC: Caused quite an excitement that did, Lord Ern of Peterborough catching a ball. My connections with sport are mostly on the charity side now.

I'm a member of the MCC and the Lord's Taverners. If I join anything, I do it properly. I won't join and not do anything. There are certain things that I am president of on paper, especially locally, that I never go to. But I warn them of that before accepting an office. I'm a vice-president of Luton now. I get one free seat instead of four and no aggravation. I still desperately want to see the Town go back into the First Division. I was director in Third Division, Second Division and First Division. Can't be bad. When we got into the First Division again in 1974, the players threw me into a bath – with all my clothes on. That's devotion for you. Luton is a very good Second Division team with a chance of going up to the First. I still go to matches, although not to the away games. The beauty of being a director or vice-president is that you go straight through to the players' entrance. There's a car-park there and I just walk four yards into the ground. That's a useful perk. Sport is a worthwhile means of raising money for charity, and people in show business are always involved in some charity function or other.

In 1969 we celebrated thirty years as a double act, so the Variety Club gave us three luncheons and an award. If they can find an excuse like that – or better still, if it's fifty years of showbiz or the anniversary of Ernie opening his wallet – then you get an award for it. They don't just get us there, but people like Vera Lynn, Max Bygraves and even Des, too. That way they have a show to sell – basically on the speeches – and the proceeds go to charity.

ERNIE: The money comes in from ticket sales. We did one in Birmingham and they charged £60 per person.

ERIC: And he paid it, this fella that came. There were speakers like André Previn, Glenda Jackson, Francis Matthews, Robert Morley, Robin Day and ourselves. Each did seven or eight minutes and it was sold to television.

ERNIE: They called it *Morecambe and Wise, This Is Your Lunch*.

Personally, I'd be quite happy to do without all those backscratching show business events.

ERIC: The most important thing is for the charity to get the money they need. That's what it's all about. It's like me with the Lord's Taverners, you can go to what might be the most miserable do imaginable, but if it raises £10,000, it's worthwhile.

ERNIE: The trouble with a lot of these functions is that they become competitive. People go along because they expect to see a lot of stars. The guest of honour gets up and makes a speech, and before you know where you are, there are three comedians trying to outdo each other. There are some people who make a living out of speeches – and they don't listen to what the other fellow's saying, either.

ERIC: It's their own image that is important to them. It is to us, too, for that matter. But I enjoy the Taverners because I like the game and it is a way of both raising money for charity and introducing young children to sport. It is also a means for me to say thank you for all the luck I have had.

Very few people, though, give anything to us out of their own pockets. Those who do, think in terms of £10 to £20.

ERNIE: When anyone offers £1,000, we know it's coming from somewhere else. That's company money.

ERIC: We go to W.D. and H.O. Wills, Nottingham, and ask them to sponsor a game. They say they'll do it for £10,000.

ERNIE: I'm a Lord's Taverner too and I belong to the Variety Club and SOS – Stars Organization for Spastics.

ERIC: Don't forget, the reason they ask people like Ernie or me or Vera Lynn or Dickie Henderson is to attract people to buy tickets for a table. In return, an artist will do his stint at the top table. There's a free meal, but we still have to work, and we don't like it, because our backs are too close to the wall. I am okay on spontaneity but written speeches I find very difficult. They are fine for the stand-up club comic who has perfected that line of business. Though I must say, if you don't feel you can score with other comics, then you're going to come out last from the public point of view, and if that is the case, you shouldn't enter the lists.

ERNIE: It's difficult for people outside our business to appreciate how much work goes into one of our routines. I had a call recently from somebody who said, 'Ern, how would you like to earn £50 for one hour's work?'

I said, 'Look, if it's charity, I'll do it for nothing. But if it's business, I want more than £50.' It *was* business and I wouldn't do it.

The phone rang about twenty minutes later. The same man said, 'Ern, could you give me Roy Castle's telephone number?'

Charity is as organized as show business and in many instances they send out lots of letters to try to catch the personalities. It can turn into blackmail. It is up to us to choose what we do want to do and what we don't.

ERIC: I feel that if I reach a certain target in the course of a year then I can afford to say I've done enough. I succeeded Prince Charles as President of the Lord's Taverners, and while I was in that position I raised between £30,000 and £40,000 a year. Even though I'm not President any longer I still do it, and achieve about £20,000 a year for them.

ERNIE: In fact, in those days, we were riding so high with all the big stars on our shows that people used to say, 'You'll be having Prince Charles next.' So we tried. He told us he would love to have done it, but if he did it for us he'd also have to do it for Spike and for Harry. He is an enormous Goons fan, but he said he couldn't do that kind of thing, even for them. He loves performing and we actually got him on stage with us tap dancing when we did a charity show – it was Silver Jubilee year, 1977 – at the Theatre Royal Windsor. He likes the singers, the coloured groups, the actors. He's a great man.

ERIC: But don't get the idea that Prince Charles and we are buddy-buddies, because we're not at all. But I think, outside his own circle of friends, I'm as accepted as much as anybody else. I'm on the Prince of Wales Trust and we have meetings at Buckingham Palace. Of course, I always call him 'sir'. I have met Prince Philip a couple of times and with him it's always a bit more difficult. But Prince Charles accepts you for what you are, for being a good comic, as he accepts Harry Secombe and Spike Milligan, and helps us with charity work.

ERNIE: My principal charity is giving blood. You can't give more than that, can you? They ask for money, but I say that's out. I'm a blood donor and I think that's a good thing.

ERIC: I needed blood when I was in hospital, but I wouldn't have his. Mine came from a beautiful young Scottish nurse. She gave me two pints of her blood. From under the kilt.

ERNIE: I give blood about every six months.

ERIC: He only does it for the tea. It must be marvellous to say that you've got Ernie Wise's blood. It means you're going to make money eventually.

ERNIE: It's very rich. I also actively support the Keep Britain Tidy campaign, I believe in that.

What I would like to see is a little bit more done for our own retired people, those who have spent their lives in showbiz. There's this false thing about theatre people all being madly rich and making fortunes, since they get £200 or £300 or whatever for a performance, but it's not true. We pay taxes like everybody else and not everybody reaches the top.

ERIC: We're either earning or resting and sometimes we have to turn down charities in order to work. Other times we turn down work for charity. We might be working extremely hard when suddenly we've got two weeks off and four charities to do. We've got to be there because we're the attraction.

The biggest charity event of the year is the *Royal Variety Show*. We've done four royal shows, but we don't like them because they always mean having to find something new.

ERNIE: We worked with Debbie Reynolds in the first one we ever did. I remember sitting in the audience with Bud Flanagan and a male ballet dancer came on, showing everything he'd got.

Bud said, 'Go and get me a couple of those, will you?'

ERIC: It's a terrible thing to be remembered for – that and 'Underneath the Arches'.

ERNIE: The first royal command we performed on, we chased a girl wearing a grass skirt across the stage with a lawn-mower.

There's always a risk that there's some up-and-coming comedian – and good luck to him – who's going to go up there and be brilliant and make everybody else look a bit sick.

ERIC: Of course, we do those shows for nothing. I don't mind dying in front of three thousand people. What I object to is that even if the show doesn't go down well, they still play it on television in front of millions – and in America, too, where it's called *A Night with the Queen*.

ERNIE: We're risking our livelihood.

ERIC: We might have people turning round and saying, 'Well, they've gone off a bit, haven't they?'

ERNIE: You're just damaging yourself. It's not under your control.

ERIC: That's what it all boils down to, and you've got to use special material. We did our last one in 1973 when we were Marvel and Dolores. I was the conjurer and he was the beautiful assistant.

ERNIE: That was a good one, Eric as the magician.

ERIC: And a fellow whistling every time I walked. Every time I moved, feathers came flying out of my arms and from the back of my neck.

ERNIE: And he got me into a cabinet at which he threw his knives. Suddenly a lovely girl came on. He looked at her and then he looked at me, a battered old bag. He threw the knives, killed me and walked off with the girl. Obvious, but it worked. What was funny was that those feathers were everywhere. They had a French girl singer come on after us. The poor thing had feathers everywhere. As she started to sing they were in her mouth, in her hair.

ERIC: Many years ago we used to do a routine with crisps. The stage staff hated us for it. I would eat them from a bag while Ernie was singing. He'd put his hand out and I'd put a crisp in his hand. Of course, by the end of the week, there was a great big grease mark on the stage which they could never get out. Usually we were followed by an animal act – dogs or seals or bears. The chap would say, 'Right, sit,' and the dogs would sniff and walk around as if the microphone were on heat.

They used to come off and complain, 'I wish you wouldn't do that crisp act', and we'd say, 'It's our living . . .'

Fortunately, doing royal shows isn't.

ERNIE: Talking of royalty makes me think of Flora Robson. I can see her now rehearsing a scene for our version of *Elizabeth I*. For a minute I couldn't remember my lines. Flora, a pro of the very old school – which is intended as a tribute and is not referring to a wonderful lady's age – seemed shocked.

'How could you forget them?' she asked. 'After all, you wrote it.' She really believed it was another of the plays what I wrote.

Flora was quite amazed watching us work. She said that even when she was performing she forgot she was working with us. She felt as though she were at home, watching our show on the box.

ERIC: In 1976, when we heard we were going to get our OBES, Flora said, 'You will treat this very seriously, won't you?' She's a royalist and was so proud of the time she was made a Dame, which we'd never been – even in pantomime. She said she'd had to stand and wait for about two hours. I said I couldn't do that – my legs were bad. Remember, it was before my operation. It was a typical Eric-

Morecambe-nobody-understands joke. But Flora took it very seriously, indeed. 'Oh, leave it to me,' she said.

She wrote to her friend – the Queen Mum! So when it came to the day of the investiture, Ernie and I and a very old man who was at least 106 were in a room just off the throne room at Buckingham Palace while everyone else was queuing up for their gongs. Flora had got us into a little ante-room where we could sit down while old men twice our age were walking past us, yards at a time.

ERNIE: The fellow who was in charge of it all was a tall colonel, very military, really handsome, standing about seven feet four high and one foot wide. He was to put us through our paces.

'Gentlemen', he said, moustaches bristling, 'when it comes to your turn for the presentation, you are going to get your medals together. Her Majesty would like that. But I think you ought to get it right.' So he stood in front of us and we began to rehearse – together, as a trio. 'As the band begins to play, you will walk forward ...' And he proceeded to demonstrate.

The three of us were going round and round this little ante-room, the seven foot four colonel singing as he went 'Bring Me Sunshine' with his full gear, his red uniform, his clanking medals. That's one the cameras missed!

ERIC: It's true. There was Ernie next to him. He could just about see the man's knee-caps. The seven-footer was singing 'Bring Me Sunshine' while we followed. He showed us what to do, dancing in front of Ernie. Fred Pontin was getting his knighthood at the same time. He was in the queue. It must have seemed like Butlins to him.

ERNIE: But when it came to the moment for them to play our music, we didn't have the fellow with us any more. We had to remember to do 'Bring Me Sunshine' as he had taught us. Everybody smiled and a little murmur went round the room. I don't think they'd ever had two men receive their OBEs together before. The music was just right – better than it was for another old chap getting a medal: as he approached the Queen, the band played 'You'd Be Far Better Off in a Home'.

You know what's nice about going to Buckingham Palace? It's being waved through by a policeman at the gate. You're expected to wear a grey topper, but you can't really wear it in the car because it gets tangled around your ears. You have to open the sun-roof. Then when you get to the Palace, they don't let you wear it inside either.

82

They even take your medal away as soon as you get it. The Queen gives it to you, pins it on and then, as you walk away, another colonel's sweaty hand grabs it and puts it in a little box containing a card telling you where you can buy miniatures. I vaguely remember the Queen saying something like:

'Thank you very much for all the happiness that you've given the people.'

That's what a lot of folks say, but we try to remember to reply, 'Thank you, but we do get paid for it.'

ERIC: The great thing about the award was the way people were genuinely thrilled for us. There was one Labour MP though, Doug Hoyle, who said, 'It's a mockery of our system of society.'

ERNIE: What he didn't realize was that the OBE is not the 'Order of the British Empire' but 'Old Butlins Entertainers'.

Eric said he regarded it as a great honour: 'I'll wear it on State occasions, like Luton Town home games.'

I've worn mine a couple of times, and I've got a miniature.

ERIC: What Doug Hoyle's really asking is, should Sir Laurence Olivier be made a Lord? Should Bernard Delfont be made a Lord?

ERNIE: They don't give too many of those in show business, anyway. Things like knighthoods go to actors but almost never to comics, except in the days of Harry Lauder and George Robey.

ERIC: I don't see a Sir Ronnie Barker. I don't see Sir Eric Morecambe or Sir Ernie Wise, either, for that matter. If that kind of thing did happen, I think it would have to be on retirement.

ERNIE: I would like to become a lord. I'd like that allowance they get every day for going to their own show at the House of Lords.

8

Milestones

ERNIE: I remember I was interviewed on *Nationwide* when I was fifty. That was in 1975. Everybody seemed to be interested in that magic figure. I wasn't. I didn't feel any different then or now. Just so long as I can keep my weight down and remain active, that's all that matters.

ERIC: Being fifty meant absolutely nothing to me. It didn't make any difference whatsoever. But I think sixty will be a milestone; I'll be more grateful to have made it, for a start. I remember as a youth thinking that a man of sixty was ancient. People were very old at fifty when I was a boy.

Of course, you do feel that little bit older when you look in the mirror for the first time and see the grey coming through the heavy black stubble that used to make you look so strong and virile. That's when you turn to page three of the *Sun* and it doesn't do anything for you.

ERNIE: When your heart starts pounding from switching on the television. And the fire's gone out and there's no coal left in the cellar. We did a sketch about looking old at around the time we both turned fifty. Eric kept asking, 'Are you on the gee-up tablets?' The grey hair still fascinates me, although I have to say that when I look in the mirror, I don't even see it. There must be something wrong with me. Actually I first started going grey when I was forty-five. I'm now more grey than Eric is.

84

ERIC: Since you bought the last wig – but I'm losing mine.

ERNIE: He's got a grey head.

ERIC: My mother said I would come out on top, and she's right.

ERNIE: Actually I use that Grecian 2,000. I certainly look like a 2,000-year-old Greek. Groucho Marx was once asked, 'Are you still chasing those girls?' and he said, 'Only if they're running downhill.'

The classic which has never been beaten is: 'It now takes me all night to do what I used to do all night.' It's still one of the best lines.

ERIC: But I do worry about being sixty. After that age I don't think it matters any more. Anything after sixty-five is a bonus, career-wise. And most important, you can travel on the buses free. Don't think Ernie won't.

ERNIE: Me and Max Bygraves.

ERIC: He's doing it now, isn't he?

ERNIE: I'm conscious of getting old, though, which one really mustn't be. It's a state that you can get into, and a dangerous one at that. I remember I used to say I didn't want to get old. I'm not looking forward to it; I don't like what I see. I'm hoping I can avoid it, but I don't know how. The truth is, I don't want to get all twisted up. It's a question of health, rheumatism and all that. When I look at some of those old folks' homes stuffed with geriatrics, I find it very depressing. We're lucky, very lucky.

ERIC: But there are still millions of people to whom we're not old. I always say that I don't want to carry on doing 'What do you think of it so far?' when I'm sixty-five. But if they're still going to laugh at it, we should. We have the advantage of being in the public eye constantly, so the audience watches us get older. They don't suddenly look at us one day and say, 'Hey, hasn't he got bald? or 'Isn't Ernie white?'

ERNIE: People used to meet me when the television sets were all black and white and say, 'I didn't know you had grey hair.' They'd always thought I was blond.

It would be marvellous if we could find two fellows who are about twenty-one and look exactly like Eric and me and then send them out on tour. We'd pay them a nominal fee, of, say, £50 a week joint.

ERIC: We'll also supply the train fares and the digs.

ERNIE: The pay-off is – if they flop, expose them. We stayed in some digs once and the woman said, 'We had your fathers with us in these digs and we've got their autographs and pictures.'

She was talking about us. I didn't know quite whether to be flattered or insulted.

'That was us,' I said.

'What?' she asked. 'In 1948?'

'Yes,' I said, 'it was me and him.'

We told Eddie about it and he did a whole routine on it:

'I'm Ernie Wise Jnr, you probably remember my father, he used to go round with an old comedian.'

'Hello, I'm Eric Morecambe Jnr. My father was a big star in his day.'

ERIC: And then Ernie said, 'My father was better than your father.'

ERNIE: It was a nice angle; because we'd been around for so long, we thought we'd come on as our own sons.

ERIC: People who say that Morecambe and Wise have the ideal partnership are absolutely right. We never have fights – although it wouldn't be true to say that we don't have disagreements. That's only healthy, surely. Basically, Ernie does the business and I do the comedy, but we do listen to each other.

I think even the impressionists understand that. They say that impersonation is the sincerest form of flattery and I suppose it's true than when they start copying you, you've arrived. Audiences love impressionists, but satisfying the subject of those impersonations is a different game of Luton Town altogether.

Mike Yarwood is very, very good. He wears a hat, which obviously means he doesn't have to wear a bald wig. But he also has the glasses – my trademark. The reason he doesn't do Ernie is because Ernie doesn't pay him. He does things with me that even I don't know I do. Perhaps that is really the secret of my success, the little things that I don't know that I'm doing. He'll know where to put the emphasis on certain words.

ERNIE: But if you've got Mike Yarwood with Eric he doesn't look at all like him.

ERIC: Oh no.

ERNIE: But Mike Yarwood could work with me as Eric and succeed beautifully.

ERIC: Johnny Ammonds, our producer, reads for me when I'm not at rehearsals and he'll think he's doing an impression of me. But he's not, because my intonation is entirely different. We've worked with him for twenty-five years, but he always sounds like Johnny Ammonds because he puts all the intonations in the wrong places. Ernie and I have a sort of telepathy, though, and the emphasis is always right.

ERNIE: Sometimes I only have to look at him and he knows exactly what gag I'm going to come out with – and how to top it.

In some shows the producer is all powerful. With us, everything is a committee decision. We want Johnny Ammonds to take the pictures for us as well as help us with the words and make other decisions.

ERIC: We couldn't do it without him, but *we* make the decisions at board meetings.

ERNIE: It's a foursome really, us, our producer and Eddie the writer – Johnny Ammonds acts for us as a kind of buffer. If we don't think a gag is going quite right, we ask Johnny to give Eddie a ring and ask him if he can change it – and he does. We don't do that ourselves because we don't want to get involved. Johnny is good because he sits in with us and makes us learn the script. I think if I were an actor who was going to do a difficult play with a great deal of dialogue I would hire somebody with a big whip to make me learn the lines. I've got to be made to do it, otherwise I'll find excuses not to do so. And it can be so hard – not only learning the current production, but also lines for the Christmas shows – that I end up going home with a terrible headache.

ERIC: The only thing I know is that when we work with Eddie Braben in any shape or form, it works.

ERNIE: But we could never do word for word what a writer had written. We have to put our own stuff into it. It's no criticism of the writer, but we feel we can improve it in places. It's very hard to get the perfect script.

ERIC: We'll only get that in heaven. St Peter will be at the gate waiting for us and he'll say, 'Read that.' If we read it and it's perfect, we're there, but he might say, 'Sorry, you've fluffed.' We never knock scripts with a hatchet, though.

ERNIE: It's a question of refining and editing.

ERIC: The only thing we'd ever row about is a script – but we don't because we've got more sense. It happened in our 1980 series that Johnny and Ernie got hold of a script and said, 'We don't think it's funny.'

But I stood my ground. 'It's hilarious,' I said, 'You've only got to add a little thing there and take out something there.'

Johnny read my part and did all his wrong intonations, but when I did it, it was right – or almost right. I know that I'm correct because I know what makes me laugh and I know that I can make others laugh with it.

ERNIE: I think that without Eric's comedy we wouldn't have got as far as we have and without my business acumen I don't think we would have done as well. It's a good combination.

ERIC: And that's it in a nutshell.

ERNIE: But he also helps business-wise and I also help comedy-wise. Our partnership works for us as it used to work for Laurel and Hardy.

ERIC: There is another thing which needs to be considered when you mention Laurel and Hardy. I don't know how many films they made, let's say they made seventy-five, altogether. Some of them only lasted twenty minutes or half an hour, but there were feature films as well. We've done more than that in five years. They didn't do in five years what a normal television performer would do in three. When they started, it was like early television. If you look at their early stuff, it was very stagy – probably ideas that Stan had come up with, because I don't think Olly put a lot in. If we were Laurel and Hardy, Stan would be here with the producer talking about what they were going to do and I think Olly would be out playing golf. With us, Ernie is in on the writing as well.

ERNIE: Hardy was a slightly better performer, wasn't he? He was more flamboyant and more of a character. But there are always different styles of performers. For some performers, it comes so easy. For others, it is always a hard slog. Two different kinds. It's like some people can learn lines quicker than a grocery list. Others have to work much, much harder at it.

ERIC: We're doing things now that we've never done before. I've been away for two or three days fishing at a time while doing our shows. I've never done that before.

ERNIE: We could have done it ten years ago if we hadn't been such hard workers.

ERIC: Eddie Braben also makes himself a more reasonable routine now. He starts at nine and finishes at five and only does a five-day week. He doesn't do weekends. The scripts come in the post to us as

88

before, and that's the way it should be. He'll last a lot longer doing that.

ERNIE: We did things before which are virtually impossible, but we did them. In fifty-two weeks, we slotted in practically everything you could imagine. Something had to go.

ERIC: And it was me. But I came back.

9

Focus on the Big Screen

ERIC: A lot of people said we should never have gone over to commercial television in 1978, but the point is that Thames only did to the BBC what the BBC had done to ATV. It's all for business. Bill Cotton may have called us rotten devils, or words to that effect, but there was no basic animosity. If I wrote to Bill and said, 'Well, Bill, I can't work any more, I need a couple of grand', he's going to turn round and say, 'Ask Ernie.' But he will say it in a very nice letter.

ERNIE: The main reason we left was because we wanted to make a film. The BBC were not interested. Thames agreed. We never got disenchanted with the BBC, but we had always wanted to make a film with them. We were always telling them we had an idea whereby all the big stars with whom we worked and the people who became good friends – like Robert Morley, Glenda Jackson, Vanessa Redgrave, Flora Robson, André Previn – would have done a little piece in it.

ERIC: For BBC television.

ERNIE: We wanted Flora Robson to be the cleaning lady, André Previn the music director, Robert Morley the doorman at the front, and we would do a big star thing. But we could never get it off the ground.

ERIC: The BBC like people to be slotted in and don't want you to come up with anything different. They aren't alone in this. There's no one running Kellogg's Cornflakes who is going to say, 'Hey, let's make them all soft this week.' If he did, someone's going to say, 'For Christ's sake, no, we're making a fortune as it is.'

ERNIE: 'Don't lose the pattern,' television companies say. 'There's the autumn shows, the winter shows and the spring shows.' The summer is bad for entertainment generally, except at the seaside, where you've got a captive audience. It all follows a pattern. It's simply a question of filling the spots, six or fourteen of them.

ERIC: It must be a marvellous feeling for the head of light enter-tainment to turn round and say to whoever is above him, 'We've got so-and-so and so-and-so for thirteen 45-minute shows and they're starting in the winter.' That's great. That's taken care of, isn't it?

ERNIE: We had no objection to carrying on the BBC shows in the same formula, but we wanted to do the film too. We also wanted to organize the financial side on the right lines, something which we'd failed to do in our earlier films.

In the sixties, when we made *The Intelligence Men*, *That Riviera Touch* and *The Magnificent Two* our lawyers weren't as good as those of the other people. We thought the notion of us making movies was a smashing idea. But the film companies had batches of lawyers who had drawn up contracts that for them were watertight. At that time we were earning a lot of money, most of which was going to go in tax, and we were looking for a spread of earnings. Now that is a very well-known phrase, but a dangerous one. They just don't spread very far.

ERIC: One in the hand is worth two in Shepherd's Bush.

ERNIE: We signed a contract for a certain amount of money and the rest was on a percentage basis. That was called 'deferred pay-ments'. We had a percentage of the box-office as well as of profits, but the makers said that the films never did make any profit. We don't think we ever got a proper return – particularly since the films have been on television, where we are big stars. In fact we've never seen anything at all from television sales of our picture.

ERIC: Even if the cinemas were not packed, we believe the movies made enough cash.

ERNIE: I'm sure that if they had to, the film companies could show concrete proof that they actually lost money. It was something we knew nothing about. You know that a live theatre seats, say, two thousand people at £5 a time, which means a minimum of £10,000 coming into the box-office. On average it will be a lot more, because some seats cost £8, so you can say that theatre's going to take in £12,000. You know how much the production is going to cost, you know how large the theatre's percentage is and you know what's going to be left. But about the money made by the films – we knew and we got nothing.

ERIC: All we ever got from them was hammered. Critics still say, 'Morecambe and Wise are in this film – a shame that they never did make the transition from small screen to the big.' And yet it happened all of sixteen years ago.

ERNIE: That's where films can do you more harm than good.

ERIC: The critics can say what they like about them, as far as I'm concerned, but the makers could give me a few quid – even a bad movie is going to be watched by a minimum of five million people on television.

ERNIE: Don't forget the BBC paid a lot to run them. Money's changing hands, and it ain't coming our way.

ERIC: We know those films were too static for us. But let's face facts: they weren't that funny. We must take the blame as well. The director would say, 'Run down that corridor and fall down, that always gets a laugh.' But it never did with us.

ERNIE: The pictures were all the same. We were caught up in something that was bigger than us that wasn't under our control. One of the problems was due to the fact that there was no audience. We were talking into a void all the time. It was too big for us.

ERIC: We never got enough practice either.

ERNIE: To become good you have to stay with it. Peter Sellers discovered that. He wasn't very good in his first pictures. We weren't good either when we were on television for the first time. We flopped. But we came back again and again. If we had gone on making films in the sixties we might be very successful film comedians. But we didn't know the medium then, and we have never had a chance to get to know it.

ERIC: Given the right script, I feel I could do anything funny on any medium, and I'm talking in the singular. I know it sounds terribly big-headed, but you need to be that to have the drive. Walter Matthau found that out. And he's a very funny man in films. Handled and directed properly I feel I could be just as funny. Don't tell me that Ernie and I, with the right director, couldn't have done

Some Like It Hot. Don't tell me we couldn't have done *The Odd Couple.*

ERNIE: *The Odd Couple* – that's Eric and me.

ERIC: If we had Neil Simon writing for us and Billy Wilder directing, I know we could be international stars. Without that though, we would have no future.

I guarantee that somewhere there's a young comic now, an eighteen or nineteen-year-old unknown, who has just started working the clubs. He *has* to think that he is going to follow Bob Hope or Jack Benny or Frankie Howerd or Morecambe and Wise ... he has to think he can do it because, if there are any doubts at the back of his mind, he'll never be very good. But there's a nice way to do it. You don't hit people, you just go home and work on it and have a couple of heart attacks.

ERNIE: There isn't a professional in show business who doesn't think – even if he is sixty-five and still on the bottom rung of the ladder – that he isn't going to make it big tomorrow. Great hopes. Tomorrow there will be a phone call ...

ERIC: And it's: 'Look, we've got this little part ...'

ERNIE: Look at George Burns, bigger than ever he was. But again, if you want to be big, really big, you've got to do it in America. Like Donald Pleasence.

But it's easy to get disillusioned. I still think the greatest moment I remember in show business was when we began work on our first film, *The Intelligence Men.* I can see the way things happened to this day. I was certain I was now going to become that international film star. We were shooting our first scene on location and they gave me a caravan. That was status, to start with. I walked into the van and discovered there was neither heating nor running water. I stayed there while my stand-in pushed my dinner through the window on a paper plate.

ERIC: I had to eat in the dressing-room at Pinewood. Come five or six o'clock or whatever the time was when we finished, I would go round to each of the major stars working there – Warren Mitchell was on the film with us and Tony Curtis was working on another picture at the studios at that time – and say, 'Come in and have a drink.' But they were all working. They used to go home with their make-up on when they had finished. They never drank with me. The only one who did was Michael Caine, who was doing *The Ipcress File*

93

at the time. I remember vividly how he stood at the door and wouldn't come in. It was as though he thought I was going to attack him, but all I did was ask him to have a drink.

ERNIE: We thought that it would be like the old Hollywood days when all the stars sat around and were buddy-buddy with each other.

ERIC: But they don't do that any more. Those days have gone. Gone! I had to sit in the bar on my own, waiting for the traffic to ease off before I could go home. We never did use all that booze, the champagne, the whisky, the gin, the wine. Tragedy! Tragedy!

Now we've got our new film written. It was one of the reasons that I had the heart-attack, because writing it was a hell of a strain. But we will get it off the ground before long. It's all in our contract with Thames and we'll do it when we are ready.

ERNIE: The BBC didn't have the set-up for it. They don't have that sort of speculative money to put into making a film. They aren't in the cinema business, but Thames is.

In our first three films, we were swamped by the manufacturing process and by the writers, who used to bring the script in on the backs of envelopes. It was a lot of fun, but that isn't enough.

ERIC: People keep telling us you can't transform from very good television to very good films. That's a load of rubbish – of course you can. The writing's got to be right; the production has to be right; the direction has to be right. It's not just a question of getting two comics or a comedian and saying, 'It's got to be right because he's a funny man.'

ERNIE: They never got it right with Sid Field, who was a great comedian. On screen he was a disaster.

ERIC: We're exactly the same in the film we're planning as we are in the flat routines in our shows. But there's a story to it, with Ernie and I as Morecambe and Wise (not as two performers who can't perform, but as two very good double-act comedians). It is based on my hobby of doing all those competitions in the newspapers and I eventually win. The prize is a part in a film with a Hollywood star; it's a double prize, so Ernie would play the part of the wife (although he doesn't dress as a woman).

ERNIE: The idea is to get somebody like Vincent Price and an American woman star – who would of course fall in love with me – so that we can get a sale in the States.

ERIC: But we wouldn't adapt our dialogue. The others can do that.

94

ERNIE: They can be Americans and we can be English.

ERIC: We can't walk about saying, 'Hi there, I'll see you on the sidewalk.' If it sells in America, fine. If it doesn't, hard luck. I'll go back to the competitions and the pools. Actually, it took years before I stopped doing them. Monday, Tuesday and Wednesday it was 'Don't forget to do the pools' and Wednesday, Thursday, Friday, it was always 'What are we doing when we've the £75,000?' One always felt it was the money you'd get for not working. It would be like having twins, you get paid twice for one performance.

ERNIE: Last year's pleasure – with lungs. I can't be bothered, though that is pure idleness. I'm really not interested in filling in the coupon and posting it and all that rubbish. I just can't do it. Eric enjoys it. We did it together at one time. We were dreaming of making a fortune.

ERIC: Without work. I still sometimes do them – the very cheap system – eight draws out of fourteen or fifteen, something like that. It's a perm.

ERNIE: Eight draws was the magic thing.

ERIC: I don't think my mother had eight draws in all her married life.

ERNIE: What was the line, a Suzette Tarry-type joke, 'I didn't get my draws off in time' or 'my draws let me down'? There was always the little dog doing his pools.

ERIC: It would make a lovely scene in our film.

ERNIE: In addition to that movie, we would like to make an hour-long television film. We're always on the look-out for the chance of doing something different.

ERIC: We can't do a two-hour show, but we can do an hour based on our flat routine. We would start off in the flat and from there go out into a situation. That would lead to another idea and the whole lot would combine into a small story.

ERNIE: After all, that is just what happened in 1978 when we did *The Sweeney*. That worked. The Sweeney were involved in an investigation at the Lakeside Club where we were supposed to be doing cabaret. We got caught up in the affair and it turned out beautifully. The really funny part about it was the night the episode was shown on television, the Lakeside Club burned down. There's a coincidence for you.

But the television companies would love us to do the same thing, the half-hour series and the Christmas show – until we dropped dead. We want to do something just to vary it, in case we fail. We haven't failed yet, but we always feel that we might. And other people feel it, too.

I suppose they felt it most when we moved to Thames. It wasn't an easy move for us. It seemed that everybody was saying, 'Are they going to be as good now as they were with the BBC?'

ERIC: We still get letters asking why we left the Beeb. I have three enormous friends, a whole family in Hampshire, and I was shattered by their reaction. Three years after we had moved to Thames the lady of the family turned round and said, 'I'm shocked that you left the BBC.'

ERNIE: It's more than that. They consider that BBC represents quality and commercial television is rubbish.

ERIC: If the BBC made us the right offer we would in all probability go back.

ERNIE: The point we're trying to make is that we are in business. We are in the marketplace and we have never belonged to anybody.

ERIC: What's wrong with working, for instance, for Granada television? Or Cumbria, Anglia or Southern? It's still Morecambe and Wise with our scriptwriter Eddie and producer Johnny Ammonds. And we will always want to do our best.

10

A Change of Heart

ERNIE: It all looked so good. The ratings had never been better and nothing, it seemed, was going to stop us – and then in January 1979 came Eric's second heart attack.

ERIC: My blood pressure went down to hardly anything. I was in a terrible way when they got me to St Albans Hospital, but I was lucky. I had a marvellous doctor who, with George Apthorpe, the specialist, got me out of it. After two weeks I thought it was all going to be great.

ERNIE: I suppose it'll be my turn next.

ERIC: He's so near the ground, he hasn't far to fall. But I wouldn't wish one on him. Heart attacks are vicious. Tachycardias are nothing in comparison. I had three tachycardias in February. I didn't feel very well, the heart-beat was going triple time – but after two heart attacks I knew what was going on. Your heart beats, beats, beats – it moves so fast you can see it under your pyjamas. I refused to go to hospital for the last one because I knew the press would grab hold of the story, so I had it at home. Nobody knew about that one.

ERNIE: When people asked me about him I said: 'He opened the fridge and the light came on. He did ten minutes of patter, didn't get any laughs and collapsed.' His attack was inevitably going to make news.

ERIC: I didn't want that kind of news again. I'd been through it all before. But the doctors said I should see Magdi Jacoub, the Egyptian surgeon who had done some marvellous tricks with hearts, although I didn't fancy seeing what he could do with spades. It was wise to find out why I'd been having heart trouble, and not just since the attack in 1968. After all, the doctors had first noticed it when I was fighting in the underground during the war. I was what they used to call a 'Bevin Boy', conscripted as a miner, which wasn't much easier than working the Glasgow Empire. They invalided me out with a weak heart when I was eighteen, but until 1968 I'd never given it a thought.

Mr Jacoub said that unless I had an operation there'd be nothing left for me. I had started writing a novel after my second heart attack, and I wanted to finish it. Mr Jacoub wasn't exactly encouraging; he said something about not listening to any long-playing records or starting any serials. Then I had to undergo an angiogram – they pushed something inside and I could see my heart on a television screen. Not much of a show as it turned out, except that the doctors could see the mess one of the valves was in. I didn't think much of it: the picture on the screen seemed so distant from the real me.

ERNIE: He'd only seen his face on the screen before and if that didn't frighten him, nothing would.

ERIC: It was after seeing that show – it wouldn't even have beaten Des O'Connor in the ratings – that I was told I had to have something done or I wouldn't live. It was as simple as that.

ERNIE: He told them he was rehearsing for pantomime and didn't have any good digs, so would they fit him in.

ERIC: That's right. 'What are you doing this afternoon?' I said, and they made their plans. Although I hadn't been really frightened I could remember the pain of the heart attacks. I just wanted it to stop, then fall asleep. If I woke up again, great. If I didn't, well, I'd never know. Anyway, two weeks later, I was in hospital at Harefield. There was no shock about going there. The shock was for Joan. What was more, it turned out that it wasn't nearly as painful for me as the kidney-stones which I'd had out in 1976. Take a tip: never get those.

ERNIE: Seventy-six kidney-stones led the big parade . . . Val Doonican had those.

ERIC: He's had so many that the first four rows of bricks in his house come from his kidneys. They're terrifying.

98

But I wasn't afraid of the heart operation, which they were going to do four days after I went into the hospital. When the big day came, I had every confidence it was going to work out well. I remember being given the happy pills at about seven o'clock. I put on the costume and had a wee before I went. They put me on the stretcher, started wheeling me down and that's all I remember.

I woke up in intensive care. That's the hard part. You've got that long tube down your throat. There's a lung machine doing everything for you because you don't actually breathe yourself, and I was on that for three days. And on antibiotics, too. Oh, those antibiotics! They gave me diarrhoea. Which wasn't at all funny when you consider that there was an appendage to every part of my body, on the private parts and the not so private parts. They were on my fingers, on my toes, up my throat, up my nose, up my ... I felt like Pinocchio before he got rid of the strings. When I got the diarrhoea, they had to unattach me ... then an hour later, I'd have to go again. Terrible.

Funnily enough, I was always able to rationalize it and say that it was merely a question of the next ten minutes. If I could get through the next ten minutes, I'd manage another ten and so on. I'm that sort of person.

The worst time was when Joan came in to look at me the day after the operation. I nearly tore everything off. I didn't want her to see me like that. I forbade her to come any more, but she did – and I remember it very vividly because she was wearing my favourite dress. No, not my *favourite* dress actually, because I was wearing it. . . . That day she stood and looked at me for about eight seconds, saw the agitation I was in, and left, crying.

About four days later, they took the tube out of my throat and it all started getting that little bit easier. I was in intensive care for about nine days, but I don't really remember more than about eight hours of it. I remember a bowl of flowers coming in from Harry Secombe and giving it to a black sister who had her eye on it. And then there were thousands of letters – I never realized I'd borrowed so much money!

ERNIE: I knew, of course, and that's why I didn't go to the hospital to see him. I didn't want the media to get busy. They'd already been camped outside the hospital – and neither of us blame them for that, except that I wasn't too pleased to hear about the bloke who tried to take a picture of Eric walking with a stick. Later, I went to his house at Harpenden when he was convalescing.

ERIC: It's a miracle, really. The operation hadn't been invented when I had my first heart attack in 1968. But I'd lasted for another eleven years, and by the time it was all over, they'd begun calling it the Eric Morecambe operation. The one I feel sorry for is Ernie, because nobody any more asks him how he is. They keep saying, 'How's Eric?'

ERNIE: I started wearing a badge saying, 'How's Eric? He's much better.' Then I put on another that said, 'But *I'm* not feeling too good.' Sometimes I tell people, 'Go over and chat to him', and they look very sheepish. They don't seem to believe he's recovered.

ERIC: I certainly do – every time I change clothes and see the four and a half miles of bad road up and down my body. The doctors say, 'Forget it.' Well, they may, but I can't. Nor can I really forget the people in show business who would have benefited by an operation like mine, like Arthur Haynes, Sid James, Freddie Frinton ... good people.

I saw my operation a few months later on *Your Life in Their Hands*. I thoroughly enjoyed it. It got a few laughs here and there.

People write to me now and say they've been advised to have the same operation that I had, and what should they do? If I say yes, it places too much responsibility on me should something go wrong; if I say no, I wouldn't be true to myself. The only thing I can say is that I'm glad *I* had it. 'It's done marvels for me,' I usually add. 'I'm working now, which I couldn't have done just before I had the surgery. That has been a further bonus.'

I appreciated hearing from people who think of me as a member of their immediate circle. The feeling from the public after the second heart attack and the operation was tremendously warm, even more so than it had been after the first attack, and it was great then. They made me a star.

ERNIE: Going into hopsital makes you public property.

ERIC: There were press people there with long-range cameras aimed at the unit where I was; they were focussing on me while I was lying in bed fighting for my life.

The same thing would have applied had it gone the other way, if Ernie had suddenly been ill – and there is no reason why it won't be his turn next time. It hasn't always got to be me. It would be just as

A country scene with Michele Dotrice.

What the nun said to the actor. Or how Eric got into the habit – in the 1980 Thames series.

The way it is and as millions saw it.

Ernie with Charlie, his poodle.

Awards again – this time, care of the Water Rats at the Lakeside Club in 1977.

Receiving the Freedom of the City of London.

They both received OBEs but Eric thought his watch looked prettier.

Not bad for the boy from Lancaster Road Juniors – an honorary degree from Princess Alexandra, Chancellor of Lancaster University.

Sizing-up time at Madame Tussauds. Getting the vital statistics right as Yehudi Menuhin (on slab, right) looks on.

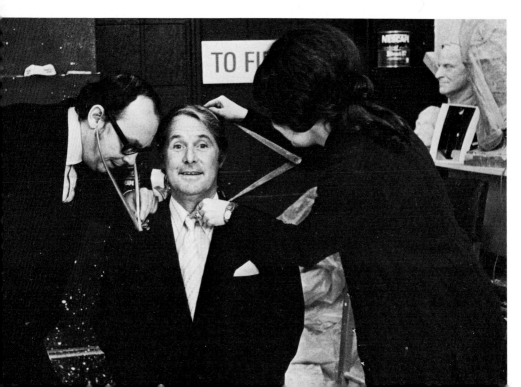

Immortality at Battersea Park after their statues had been unveiled for what was described as 'a tribute to British geniuses'.

frustrating for me to think: 'Christ – I've got these great ideas, and we can't do them.'

ERNIE: It wasn't easy for me to sit back and wait for Eric to recover, but I didn't really have much choice. A number of producers came along with ideas for shows they wanted me to do alone – like presiding at a sort of *New Faces* amateur talent programme – but, frankly, they smacked too much of disloyalty on my part to even consider them. There would be time enough to think of going it alone – if the unthinkable happened. From the time he went into hospital I just wasn't going to give it any thought.

Actually, that isn't quite true. Of course, I thought about what I would do if Eric didn't feel as if he wanted to go back to work. But, having said that, it was not a prospect I relished. We had been a double act ever since we were kids and this wasn't the time to start ringing up my agent asking him to book me as a solo. We had never lived in each other's pockets – always having our own family life, going to separate destinations on holiday – but we are close friends.

But I did know that if the worst came to the worst I could get work as a single. I could top the bill at the Palladium – once. And that was another worry. People would want to see what I was like alone, but if they didn't like what they saw, they would soon enough let me know it. So the Palladium would come later. If I was going to fall at the beginning, I hope it wouldn't be from a great height. However, I did think that anything that Des O'Connor could do, I could do too. And, of course, there were pipe dreams – of one day being another Peter Sellers, becoming the sort of actor he did.

But I didn't have to think too hard: after a year laying off – there were plenty of little things to do like opening shops and appearing at charity functions – Eric was well enough to do a short 1979 Christmas show and contemplate our new series for Thames. The operation made a new man of him.

ERIC: When I came out of hospital, it seemed that everyone wanted to see how much I'd changed. They mentioned me on the telly and printed pictures in the papers. I gew a moustache, much to the disgust of a lot of the fans. I called it my football moustache. It was eleven a side. It looked terrible. Joan liked it, but nobody else did; they said it wasn't me. When I started work again, I had to take it off. It was plain that the public really wouldn't have accepted it. But what publicity it was! Absolutely fantastic. I'm going to grow a beard next. We do so many things that we don't even dream are going to be good for PR. In this case somebody heard that I was growing a moustache, and reported and photographers were down in droves to the house wanting to take pictures.

The press have always been very good to Ernie and me and I would never knock them for their interest. They come to the house and their catch-phrases are: 'Could I have a word?' and 'Just one more!' After my operation they said, 'Look, the golf course is just at the back of the house – do you mind running up and down?'

They would have tried it if I hadn't said, 'Come on, do me a favour.'

They didn't press the point. The first time I faced them after coming out of hospital I walked into my living-room at home, and there were some twenty fellows there. I came in with my stick and moustache and said, 'Well, I suppose you're all wondering why I sent for you', and that, of course, broke the ice. We went into the garden. It was a lovely day, they took a few pictures and I opened a bottle of champagne. I must say I liked it. I love show business. I love it all, the cameras and waiting for somebody to shout, 'Cut!'

I didn't go to the Gene Kelly lunch which took place quite soon after my operation because I didn't want to break up my plans for four days' fishing. Had I gone I would only have got in two days on the river, and it was the May fly season. The press rang my house afterwards.

'Why wasn't Eric there?' they asked Joan. 'Has he had another heart attack? Is he ill? Is he in hospital?'

'No,' said Joan, 'he's fishing.'

Incredible as it may sound, the journalist then said, 'I'm sorry, we'll have to check up. We just can't believe it.'

Even so, I knew they were on my side.

The operation had been very tough on the family. It was harder on Joan than it was on me. She still had the house to run and our young son Stephen to look after, quite apart from coping with the deluge of letters. What was more, she was still limping from a broken ankle – on the night I had the second tachycardia she had tripped over our dog's harness and fallen down the stairs. On top of all this we were having the house altered, and there were builders and their chaos to contend with. When I returned from hospital I just

102

sat down quietly in the middle of it all and started writing.

ERNIE: With my being such a great playwright it was only fair Eric should have a go at being a man of letters.

ERIC: Capital letters. I wrote out my first book, *Mr Lonely*, in longhand first, then typed it with two of my best fingers, capital letters only. The only punctuation it had was asterisks and question marks.

ERNIE: He'll learn. It takes years to produce the plays what I write. Good titles, like *Mutiny on the Bonty*, only come after years at the typewriter. Seriously though, *Mr Lonely* kept him quiet when he couldn't do the shows.

ERIC: After my recuperation the only lasting physical change is that I can't pick up my legs to dance, and it hurts when I stamp my foot. There is a weakness caused by the transplanting of a vein from my leg to my heart. It will go eventually, but by then I will be too old to do a dance routine.

Ernie still worries about me. I can see he is worried first thing at rehearsals. If I'm five minutes late, there's no thought of a road accident – he is concerned lest I've had another heart attack.

ERNIE: No. What worries me is if the telephone rings between eleven at night and nine in the morning.

ERIC: He thinks it's my voice saying, 'I'm not quite dead.'

ERNIE: I know that, hell or high water, we come to rehearsals. So if he doesn't turn up, there must be something very wrong. Our work is good therapy, anyway. We keep practising, Eric and I, all the time – not like some of those fellows who just walk on and make it up.

ERIC: I'd like to meet one of those.

ERNIE: The secret of our success is practice, hard work and coming to rehearsal.

ERIC: For the 1979 Christmas show I wanted to come down on a stretcher with two ambulance men.

ERNIE: I spoke to Harry Worth soon after it. He said he'd enjoyed the show, but he wished Eric wouldn't run up and down the steps. People do get worried.

ERIC: That to me is half the fun.

ERNIE: But of course there is this great mystery of medical science; we don't understand it. It's the unknown, we are all afraid of it.

ERIC: Go on, you're going to die anyway.

ERNIE: Yes, but I want to have a crack of the whip.

ERIC: In 1980, in the middle of the Thames series, I went on the waggon to get my weight down.

ERNIE: And to rest his arm.

ERIC: The doctors said I was putting on too much. So I started drinking orange juice all day. Then when I looked at the carton and saw it contained four hundred calories, I went back to lemon tea again. Actually, I was nearer the stage where I was drinking too much for my own good, getting through a half bottle a day, mostly whisky. I had only really started drinking ten years before.

ERNIE: It's the pressure, isn't it? You've got to relax while living at great speed. I drink, but I don't *drink*, I like a glass of wine and a cigar.

ERIC: There was nothing wrong with what I was doing, but it could have become a problem if I hadn't been careful – a drinking problem. But I don't miss it.

ERNIE: You were lucky to have a doctor who prescribed a glass of whisky after a hot bath.

ERIC: And I haven't finished the hot bath yet. But there was no problem because I knew I could give it up. I've given up the pipe, too.

ERNIE: You used to smoke cigarettes.

ERIC: Yes, years ago, fifty a day and that was before I got home. I don't miss them either. I always have a cigar to chew.

ERNIE: You've got to make up your mind whether or not you are going to kill yourself. You've got to say that you've got another ten or twenty years of active life and ask if you want it.

ERIC: And after all the hard work that the doctors have done for me with the surgery, I can't let them down, can I? It wouldn't be fair.

I've been lucky, of course, and I'm the first one to admit it – lucky in my family, lucky in my work and lucky, too, in finding new interests, like my writing. Not just this book with Ernie, but writing novels.

I've seen my first novel published, *Mr Lonely*, all about a comedian who dies after being stabbed by the show business award he has craved all his life. I'd had the idea for years, but never got round to writing it. I suppose it first came to me when I read about thousands from one regiment, men recruited from Sheffield or somewhere near there, being killed during the First World War. I thought it would make a marvellous film, with Ernie and me getting killed at the end.

'You can't do that,' said the producers we approached. 'Comedians can't get killed!'

Well, why not? I thought. Comedians are human. They do die. And that's why I thought it would be a good basis for a book – the comic actually dies. But it's not all as morbid as that.

ERNIE: Comics are allowed to 'die' on stage – so long as they can walk away again.

ERIC: Well, it was an idea and the publishers liked it. Of course, I'm not worried about the risk of not making a fortune with it. There's always the soft bed of Morecambe and Wise comedy to fall back on, but I've got much more of a thrill out of the book than I ever had from a television show. I suppose, though, it's a case of the grass being a bit greener on the other side. If I were a writer, I'd want to do a television series and then think *that* was marvellous. But everyone seems as happy with the book as I am. Joan certainly is. She never thought I'd do it. I told her I would and she kept saying, 'Oh, yes ...' Well, I've proved it and she's thrilled. The only thing that worries her, I think, is the sex side – in case people think it's autobiographical, which it most definitely isn't. But she knows that, so it's all right.

One of the other nice things about it is that the publishers didn't have to make any changes in it. They just put in a few full stops and corrected the spelling, which is atrocious. I can't even spell 'spelling'.

Now I'm doing another book. In fact, I'd like to write one novel a year, writing as I go along. I'm going to tie a Biro to my left leg.

Like show business, it's all fun.

11

Hardly a Silent Night

ERNIE: We make no secret of it: the shows that mean the most to us are the ones we put out at Christmas. To many people they have become as important a part of the festive season as plum puddings and turkey. That gives us a certain sense of responsibility. Other programmes can flop – the Christmas ones must never be allowed to. Sometimes we spend a whole year gathering material for them; a quickie already filmed here, an expensive sketch with a top star planned there.

But although our Christmas shows have always been the flagships of our operation, it doesn't mean to say we will always do one. The BBC used to say, 'Okay, we'll get Morecambe and Wise to do a Christmas show.' But we're not so gullible as to agree to that now. We have to know whether we can put together a show that is of high enough quality before we start.

ERIC: We would rather offer to do a Christmas show off our own bat than be committed to one. We will accept only if we can be sure we have the basis of a show already in hand. The final decision would come in October.

ERNIE: And it is only in these last two years that we've been contracted to Thames for a set amount of shows. The BBC wanted us to do a *Morecambe and Wise Christmas Special* in 1978 and I remember Eric phoning up saying he didn't think we could get one together.

We just hadn't enough material. It was as simple as that. It doesn't mean that we wouldn't have done it had they put a great show together for us, but we couldn't manage it ourselves.

We had read through a pile of scripts, but it was obvious that we were short of ideas. We didn't have one blockbuster, which we always need, to carry the rest of the show. In the end, Michael Parkinson introduced a package of some of our best sketches and routines.

ERIC: And that was fine for us. It was a relief, their having been able to make up our minds. We didn't know they had ideas of their own, and that they were going to put a compilation together. When they announced their plan, I was happier than ever, for they had a lot of very good stuff to play with. I remember at that time saying, 'We've done enough television; perhaps we ought to stay off for eighteen months.' Of course, I had no inkling that another heart attack would make the decision for me.

ERNIE: But without a show the people would have been disappointed. I was at a dinner with the actor George Sewell once and he told me a quite amazing story that he swore was true. His family were trying to decide where to go for their Christmas holidays and finally plumped for Austria. They were going to do some ski-ing. Then, 'while we sat talking about it,' said George, 'we saw the trailer for your Christmas show. I told my wife, "If we go to Austria for Christmas, we'll miss the *Morecambe and Wise Show*." So we didn't go.' Can you imagine that?

ERIC: I think people have been feeling that way ever since our Christmas show of 1970 when Peter Cushing was on together with William Franklyn, Eric Porter, Edward Woodward – and Rex Rashley. Rex is dead now. He was a little old fellow whom we used to build up. We'd say, 'Here he comes, John Wayne', and then this little old man would walk out. I remember that particular show in 1970 because he wasn't very well, I think he had been in hospital. We were doing Robin Hood and we wanted him to play one of the Merrie Men. He came out of hospital to do it, and died soon after going back there. It was very sad. Rex did a lot with us. He was the Harpenden Male Voice Choir – just him on his own. We get hold of people like that through pure luck. It just happens, doesn't it? One day we said we wanted a little old man to play a part and he came along. I think Eddie Braben may have suggested him.

ERNIE: Usually, someone knows somebody who knows somebody

else. It's like a family concern. Sometimes, though, you want an actor to play a part but can't think of anybody. There must be thousands who would love to do it, but you just can't make that connection. We spend hours trying to think of people.

ERIC: We get the *Radio Times* and *TV Times* and look for names. Sometimes we just do it for the future – without any particular programme in mind. And we look through the acting directory *Spotlight* trying to find personalities and people we might be able to use. There could be a really big chance for somebody – a performer – who might never have considered working for us. With the sort of timetable to which we work, it's important to have people in hand.

We always tape our Christmas shows at the last possible moment. Not for our sake, but because the audience ought to be in the Christmas spirit. You can't go on in the middle of August and say, 'I've got a Christmas present for you.' The audience in the studio wouldn't accept that in the middle of summer. They're just not geared to it. Ideally, I should like to leave it even later, but the latest we've ever done it was on 17 December.

ERNIE: One of the most outstanding of all the Christmas shows must be our 1971 special. It really was the greatest. We not only had André Previn doing a Grieg piano concerto with us, but Glenda Jackson out-doing Ginger Rogers. And there was Shirley Bassey singing 'Smoke Gets in Your Eyes' wearing those boots. That combination of three big stars all together was a great moment.

ERIC: All in one show. If you had those three people in separate shows doing those things it would not have been good enough.

ERNIE: Shirley, though, can be temperamental. She is a top artist, after all. We wanted her to come to rehearsal at Delgano Way in a room which is part of a pensioners' club, full of old people singing 'My Old Man Said "Follow the Van" '. She thought we were going to come to her suite at the Dorchester to pick her up and then be entertained in the lap of luxury. When she arrived by taxi all she could say was 'You didn't even send a Rolls for me!'

ERIC: People always say, 'How did you get Shirley Bassey to wear those big boots?' It's simple. We asked her. We explained it all and she fell about and said she'd love to.

With her it was just another example of how we make our lady guests lose their dignity. We've just thought up a new one for our flat routine: we would have someone like Anna Ford come to see us, only to find that the door has jammed. So she has to talk through the letterbox to us. She can't get in, and – we're two storeys high in this flat, remember – eventually she has to get a ladder to enter through the window.

ERNIE: It really would be a good idea for a Duchess – perhaps we can persuade the Duchess of Marlborough or someone.

ERIC: Of course if they actually did lose their dignity, then we wouldn't get laughs.

ERNIE: Of our male guests, André Previn was the one who we have to put right at the top of our list. He agreed to do a show, came in on the Friday before it and everything seemed marvellous.

ERIC: That was until he told us he was going off to Los Angeles that day. We were due to tape the show the following Tuesday.

ERNIE: We managed to grab him some time before he left, give him the script and then talk it over with him. But when he said he was going to Los Angeles, we nearly had a fit. We thought L.A. meant Luton Airport.

ERIC: We asked 'When will you be back?'

'Monday,' he replied.

We went white. We were doing it on the Tuesday with a rehearsal on Monday. That was when we had a fight with our producer, Johnny Ammonds.

'I don't want to do it, I don't want to know about this,' I said. 'It's long speeches and there's a lot of it, a ten-minute piece.'

ERNIE: You couldn't make these things up, after all. He was going to be conducting his music in it. Come back on Monday? We knew he wouldn't. But on the Monday afternoon, André was in the studio and knew it better than either of us did. He was word perfect.

'How on earth did you manage to learn it?' I asked him.

'Well,' he said, 'I studied it in the back of the cab coming here. It must have been getting dark, I had to use a torch!'

ERIC: That's how he learnt it – and with not one fault, absolutely marvellous.

ERNIE: Could have been a great actor.

ERIC: The Americans have that.

ERNIE: If we had half the confidence that the Americans have got – they're sensational in that department – then we'd be bigger stars than we are. With André's delivery of lines, his looks, he's really got it. He could be a great actor today.

ERIC: Tonight.

It turned out to be one of the best sketches we've ever done. I was a concert pianist playing Grieg's piano concerto like a kid learning 'Chopsticks' and André was conducting the big orchestra.

When he complained that I wasn't playing the Grieg he knew, I told him, 'Yes, but we've rearranged it. We've jerked it up a bit.'

It was like working with one of the great American comedians. His timing was superb.

ERNIE: The concept for the sketch originally came from Hills and Green, but Eddie Braben rewrote it. At first, I was going to be the conductor and Eric was to play the pianist. Then we came up with the idea of using some big composer or other. A lot of names were suggested, but André was the one we really wanted. That again is very important, to have our real first choice, not a substitute.

We really didn't need any actual musical knowledge to do the sketch. The same sort of musical jokes would have been incorporated in a sketch with Beethoven or Brahms. Musically, it was totally wrong anyway.

ERIC: I didn't need any skill. Everyone knows that Grieg was Norwegian. I thought I'd phone him, but I was afraid he might be out ski-ing.

ERNIE: The sketch was expensive, of course. We had a full orchestra who only played three chords. It cost a fortune, but they had to be paid, all those fellows in their penguin suits going 'ding'. You can't do it any other way with a comedy about a symphony orchestra.

ERIC: You can't put dummies out there.

ERNIE: But you can do whatever you want to do and get the money for it just so long as the end product succeeds.

With the larger Christmas shows we had to have more sketches. It was more work, but of course we used to do it in less time. In those days, we did one day with the audience and probably had another single day in the studio or in two studios – if that.

ERIC: The 1972 Christmas show wasn't so successful. We were rehearsing in a restaurant with Susan Hampshire when I collapsed with flu. I ended up being taken home by Bill Cotton. Himself.

ERNIE: All we could do that Christmas were the music numbers with Kenny Ball and one little routine fortunately saved from the dress rehearsal when Bill Cotton said, 'Quick – get a channel and record that bit.' He knew Eric was finished for that year. I don't think we even had a stand-up.

ERIC: We had to do a show of some kind that Christmas because even without completing it, it would have cost the BBC between £15,000 and £20,000. They buy their own studio space. They employ people too – and all the artists and musicians have to be paid.

ERNIE: A Christmas show today must cost up to £60,000 or even £80,000. But that has to be kept in perspective with the twenty-six million people we could expect to have viewing us.

ERIC: The rest of the year, just so long as we do four good shows out of the six in a series, we can afford to lose the other two. We would hide them, by putting them in the number three and number five spots. If the others – particularly the last – are good, then we still did a great series.

But in 1972, even the Christmas show couldn't be great. Apart from the new bits, the material was pinched from stuff that was already in the can, but not due to go out until the series that followed the Christmas show. When I was fit again after the flu, we came in and did extra items to make up for the cannibalized sketches. The sketch we had planned to do with Susan Hampshire was taped later in the year – but this time with Diane Cilento in Susan's role because she couldn't make it on the second date.

ERNIE: Yes, that was also in a play what I'd written. Later, Susan came on and did another show – this time a *King Kong* sketch. She played the professor's daughter.

ERIC: I was the newspaper writer. It was the best thing that Eddie Braben had written for us to date. We were supposed to be four storeys up in this room with big windows. We put a very large picture of a chimp behind the glass – King Kong himself who had just destroyed London. As I opened the curtains I saw those big, brown eyes looking at me.

'Have we got a new window cleaner?' I asked. It was a great line.

And then there was the gag about the legs. We went to an island to look for King Kong. We had two huge bow legs built, big hairy things. Without realizing it, we were sitting on one of its feet, and as I was lighting my pipe and striking a match, I suddenly looked up and saw we were right between his legs. I said to Susan, 'Don't look up, you're too young.'

She screamed, but you couldn't see anything, it was all imagination.

ERNIE: We had a table and a chimpanzee and, if I'm not mistaken, it disgraced itself in the middle of a shot, didn't it, all over St Paul's?

ERIC: That was nerves. I just get a dry lip.

ERNIE: I know we were furious because we don't allow ad-libbing in our shows.

ERIC: That's perfectly true, but I think all that kind of thing should be kept for the archives. I don't know whether the BBC kept it or burnt it. I think it's great.

ERNIE: We're always looking for new comic ideas, never resting on our laurels.

ERIC: Or our Hardys. But we can only do things our way. There are certain things that stick in people's minds, like Angela Rippon dancing or Shirley Bassey's boots. But there are others that we've done which no one remembers – and there's nobody more surprised than we are.

Ernie has this marvellous expression: 'When you've done the best that you can ever do and you've got the biggest laughs that studio ever heard and Eric is as funny as he's ever going to be and I am as good as I'm ever going to be and the public say, "Not so good", then you know it's time for the walking shoes to go on.'

ERNIE: That's when we know they've got fed up with us. They've had enough.

ERIC: The only ones who will watch us then are the people who are going to have the operation that I've had. They turn round and say, 'You see, he's had it and can do it, so can you.' It's true, perfectly true. But we keep on, with new ideas and new plans. And there are times when we don't think we've done so good, but people tell us it was the best routine in the whole series.

We never try to irritate our audiences. We're not trying to annoy them in any way or hurt them. We're simply trying to entertain. Nobody goes out of his way to be deliberately bad. In fact, we try very, very hard.

ERNIE: In the Christmas show of 1977 we tried so hard that I think we hit the jackpot of all time. We did the 'There's Nothing like a Dame' routine from *South Pacific* with a group of television personalities dressed up in white American sailor uniforms – Richard

Baker, Frank Bough, Richard Whitmore, Barry Norman, Eddie Waring, Philip Jenkinson, Michael Parkinson and Michael Aspel all doing wonderful somersaults – and finally a very tall, weary-looking Peter Woods joining them 'singing' the final chorus in an attempted low voice.

That was the show we also had Angela Rippon and Penelope Keith, to say nothing of Francis Matthews, Richard Briers, Paul Eddington, Elton John, James Hunt and all the cast from *Dad's Army*. That was one hell of a cast.

They don't get that many in a command performance. Just occasionally we've wanted to bring in non-actors to play parts – and the effect has rebounded through the English-speaking world. We thought we had a superb idea for a Christmas show. We were casting the top union leaders – Tom Jackson, Jack Jones, Clive Jenkins and Len Murray – in a military scene we were going to do with *The Sweeney*. It seemed a good idea, because at the time there were an enormous number of things going on with the unions and we thought it would prove very popular.

ERIC: Ernie and I would have been captured prisoners about to be shot. All that would have been seen at first on the screen would have been the point of a gun. Then the picture would have opened out and it would be clear that behind the rifles were Jenkins, Murray, Jackson and Jones in German uniforms. When we asked them they all wanted to do it. But without any warning, a chap from the Bedford area complained.

'I'm an Equity member,' he said. 'They aren't. Why can't I be in this?'

So all the union leaders, God rest their souls, panicked and ran. They didn't want any trouble whatsoever. They said they couldn't do it because they were all in the South of France and in the Bahamas that day. This fellow Donald Ducked the whole thing. So we had to get a better gag; we used Des instead.

ERNIE: We finished up using four pictures of the men – as a sort of throw-away.

ERIC: Actually Clive Jenkins did come and see the show – and laughed. In all the wrong places.

I think Des flew from Australia to do the gag, but it meant he could get in Christmas at home.

ERNIE: And get the air fare back. We now had to use five men instead of the four with Des as the fifth. He didn't wear a helmet, I might add. He wasn't going to spoil his lovely blond hair.

ERIC: That Equity idiot won because he made us use five other men, but thank God – in my opinion, anyway – he wasn't one of them. That man stopped twenty million viewers from having a good laugh at Clive Jenkins and all the others, and he didn't earn a penny from it himself. If I ever found out his name, as far as I'm concerned he'd be a closed shop. The BBC had to pay for Des O'Connor triple what those four union men would have earned. They could have got 3p each and given it all to their unions!

ERNIE: They would have got a guest fee of £100 each or something. It was only a fun thing and that's how they wanted to do it – as a fun thing. It would have lasted for two or three seconds, top weight. How the row started was all a bit of a mystery to me.

ERIC: It didn't make any difference to the sketch. The point is, we feel we should have the right to say 'I want *this* man.'

ERNIE: We wanted Andrew Gardner for our Christmas show. But Equity stopped that, too. We wanted him for a lovely Victorian music hall scene, but because he was a member of the News Readers' Guild or whatever it is, they wouldn't let him. So we used Nicholas Parsons instead.

That was the year we decided to ask Sir Harold Wilson to appear, which was a lot easier – because we were asking him to play himself, not a part.

ERIC: It really was very easy. He simply agreed to do it. I asked Ted Heath and he said no.

ERNIE: Harold Wilson was always that sort of a person. You immediately get a rapport with Harold. He can talk on so many subjects. With Edward Heath, I think we would have been a bit tongue-tied.

ERIC: A classic line came out of the lunch to which we invited Harold.

I said 'I might as well tell you now, Sir Harold' – you call him that instinctively – 'you are looking at the two biggest capitalists in the world.'

All he said was, 'Well, you'll learn . . .' which I thought was great.

ERNIE: We met him secretly at the White House Hotel. We waited to see how quickly it would be in the papers. It was there, the following day.

ERIC: Probably through a waiter.

ERNIE: We were trying to keep it secret and I thought we were doing a good job – and I still think that was what we did in getting him in the first place.

Of course, learning speeches is the big problem with most non-professionals. And with Sir Harold, too. When we asked him to appear, the first thing he said was he didn't want too many long lines.

The thing I remember more than anything else was walking along Lord North Street where he lived, looking for his home. Suddenly a man tapped me on the shoulder and said, 'Over here.' It seems that Sir Harold had been looking through his window, saw me walking in the wrong direction, and sent one of his men down to bring me to the house.

ERIC: We knew it was going to be difficult, but we also knew it would be worth it. I don't think there's anybody in the world who wouldn't take a prime minister or an ex-prime minister for his show if he had the opportunity. It's like saying we wouldn't want Richard Nixon on our show. Of course we would. So would Bob Hope. I don't think there is an American comic – with any sense anyway – who would turn down Richard Nixon doing a dance routine or something like that.

ERNIE: We were looking for a different idea and if having Sir Harold wasn't it, what was?

ERIC: It'll never be repeated, I can tell you that. None had ever done it before; no future ex-Prime Minister will repeat it. Everybody loved it. For an ex-Prime Minister, he was great. The first thing I said when I met him on the show was, 'It's Mike Yarwood.' He liked that.

ERNIE: We planned it all with him in mind. We worked it so that he just walked in and sat down. We didn't give him too much movement to do. Most people don't realize how difficult it is simply making an entrance, just walking into a room and sitting on a settee.

ERIC: It would be a good idea to take a secret movie of people going into a room and watch how relaxed they are. Then we would say, 'Now we are going to film you coming in and sitting down.' It wouldn't be anything like as good. They'll fall over, they'll limp, they'll smile and they'll suddenly go stiff around the legs.

ERNIE: Normally we guide them, get both sides, under the elbow.

ERIC: You can't see any of it.

ERNIE: We explain what it is all going to be about. Sir Harold made one or two suggestions of his own. 'You fell into the sea at Morecambe and were washed up at Liverpool' was one of his gags.

ERIC: I told him Luton next year will definitely be in Europe – if there's a war.

ERNIE: We kept it very light, with no politics. We would like to have Margaret Thatcher. In fact, any Tory politician who wants to come and do our show is quite welcome.

ERIC: We're waiting for volunteers. I'd love it.

ERNIE: You're making our sketch sound like a party political broadcast.

ERIC: How about Enoch Powell?

ERNIE: If we did, we'd try to keep it a secret. We failed to surprise everyone with Sir Harold; the whole story was well known before our programme was aired. There is, of course, the argument that this sort of thing heightens people's expectations but we should have liked to have done it without anyone knowing, let them see the door open and the ex-prime minister walking on.

ERIC: Occasionally, we are a bit naughty with announcements about guests. We are known as Morecambe and Lies.

ERNIE: We said we were going to have a famous Prince on the show and somebody said, 'It's going to be an Alsatian dog.'

ERIC: The whole thing was blown. It got out from the studio. Anything we want to do that should be secret always comes out. People are getting kickbacks; they're getting the Nelson Eddies. . . .

It's around October that the press start getting friendly. We know what they're after – 'who have we got in the Christmas show.' That's all they're interested in.

ERNIE: All we want to do is a comedy show that gives people a laugh.

ERIC: There was a chap from the *Daily Mirror* in the audience one time, writing up everything we did. How the hell does he know at that stage whether it's a good show? There's still a lot to do.

ERNIE: They give us the publicity, which we like when we want it, but they steal the thunder as well, because they're in the same business as we are. Surprises. When Angela Rippon was on the show, somebody took a clip off the main tape, sent a picture to a newspaper and got paid.

ERIC: I think he got a handful of readies – and then the boot. The people on the paper who paid for that particular picture tut-tutted and said, 'The BBC shouldn't do that sort of thing.' But they did do it and rightly so – even though we have to admit it was tremendous publicity. We couldn't buy that!

I don't mind the scenes getting out, but what I don't want to lose is that little special extra something. When it's all been out, you've got nothing to give them.

ERNIE: We are always willing to take people's ideas for the show – and pay for them if they are good.

My brother Gordon was put out once after he wrote a quickie for us. We didn't use it, so he sent it off to another BBC show. They did use it, but he never got any money or recognition for it.

ERIC: He'd have had double that if he had said, 'I'm Ernie Wise's brother ...' He still writes stuff for us. We don't use it, but he still sends it in.

ERNIE: Some of the funniest things we have done don't involve either of us. Like the credits for the play with Diana Rigg in 1975. 'Written by Ernie Wise, presented by Ernie Wise, story by Ernie Wise' and 'Owing to the high cost of postage, Ernie Wise would like to wish his wife and all his friends a Happy Christmas.' The show ended with the credit: 'Written by Eddie Braben – with additional material by Eric Morecambe and Ernie Wise.'

ERIC: If you can't get an original twist to a show, there really isn't much point in doing it.

That was how we came to have Elton John play on our show five minutes after it finished. Really. After the credits and the BBC globe and the copyright symbol and everything else. The show had begun with him looking for us in the Television Centre reception and for an hour he kept popping up in all sorts of places – never really taking the hint that we didn't want him. First he got lost in the lift. Then he got caught up in a routine with the cast of *Dad's Army*.

ERNIE: He went into the *News* just as Kenneth Kendall was supposed to be reading it and handed him a note saying that we had sent him there, but the best part was when he walked through a doorway straight into the Thames.

ERIC: Finally, after it seemed that the show had finished – and we had done a full hour – he found his way to a piano while Ernie and I, dressed up as a pair of scrubbers – I mean cleaners – put our legs in our wrinkled stockings over the balcony rail and listened to him play. When he finished, we went back to scrubbing the floor.

I'm not sure that having the credits before he played completely worked, because some people switched off, but they remembered to watch when it came to the repeat.

ERNIE: I met somebody afterwards and asked if he enjoyed the show.

He said yes.

'What about the bit at the end?' I asked, for we were pretty excited about it.

He said, 'What bit at the end?'

It turned out he had taped the show, but it went off after the hour was up.

ERIC: He's a nice chap, Elton. Just before he came on, Ernie said to me, on camera, 'How much does he want?'

'£35,' I said, 'and two Luton players.'

'That's about £50,' said Ernie.

I've been to see Watford play with Elton – although I have never been to his home.

ERNIE: I don't think anyone does go to his home. You have to contact him through a telex machine. The disconcerting part about him was that when he came to see us at rehearsal he always used to call us 'sir'. 'We want you to stand there,' we would say and he would answer, 'Yes, sir', and do exactly as he was told.

ERIC: He called Ernie 'Sir' and me 'Madam'.

ERNIE: But you get that with a lot of the younger people. The Beatles called us 'sir'. 'What would you like us to do, sir?' they asked and that was years ago. We felt very old. I suppose that's how we ourselves would be with George Burns or Bob Hope. We get respect, that's what it is. But it's very nice. Elton showed us his hair. There were a few little curls there. Somebody sneezed and he had to go back and have it done again.

ERIC: I don't think he had the job done on his head, I think he got Frank Sinatra's old one, an arrangement of 'My Way'.

What I liked about him was that he wasn't like Tom Jones. He didn't have a load of managers hanging around after him in a corner saying, 'You'd better not say that or do that.' Elton is his own master and that is a good thing.

And he didn't mind going on after the hour was up. Actually we never did an hour show. They always allowed us an extra five or six minutes on a Christmas show. One Christmas we were on three times. There was a normal programme, a Christmas Spectacular and a New Year show – in 1973-4. It was just the way it worked out. But we simply wouldn't allow things to work out that way now. It really was overexposure, overkill.

It's like sex – you make it last as long as possible. That's the secret. Comedy and sex go hand in hand – if you will pardon the expression. You wake up in the morning and you say, 'It's going to be another good day for comedy.'

ERNIE: We've always worked with enthusiasm, that's another secret actually. If you've got a funny bit, you can't wait to put it in front of an audience.

ERIC: Once that's gone, Mr Barclay will be very worried.

ERNIE: That's what it is; that's the secret of it all.

ERIC: And Mickey Rooney still has the same enthusiasm that he had when he first said, 'This is a lovely place. We can do a show in here.' He's a much married man, a much older man and a much fatter man, but given the right part, he'd work his cobblers off.

But the right sort of enthusiasm can only be there when you've got something good in front of you. It has to be a *great* feeling, not just a good one. You can't buy that. It's like a young fellow buying his first motorbike. We get that feeling every week.

ERNIE: Scoring a goal, isn't it?

ERIC: It's punching the air with nothing in sight. But you've got two and a half seconds to go before the final whistle.

ERNIE: We try to have that enthusiasm even if we haven't got a television series to do and it's just opening a shop. It's like a fix. There is this incredible need to perform in front of people and I've had it since I was six years of age. This isn't a job – it's a way of life. Otherwise we wouldn't do it, would we? Why do we do it? What is it, anyway, an ego trip? I don't know anything else. When we have a really marvellous idea, we're doubly elated.

ERIC: But we both have to like an idea. If either Ernie or I say, 'I don't think this is going to work', then we wouldn't do it. But we do have to talk it through – because it's only human to make mistakes. After all, we ourselves know that the best writer in this country is Eddie Braben and yet sometimes we take stuff back to him. Like shopping at Marks and Spencer. Even Eddie can't give you twenty-four hours of brilliance.

ERNIE: Asking a lot, isn't it?

ERIC: Week after week after week. Don't tell me Neil Simon hasn't ever done rubbish, because he has.

ERNIE: But of course there is such a thing as a magic pair of scissors. You can edit things out.

ERIC: Eddie doesn't sit up there in Liverpool purposely writing rubbish that he can send down to us. He sits in that office of his and he tries to get it right for Morecambe and Wise – and for himself. And if we don't rate it, we either send it all back or just parts of it and then he tries very hard to rewrite it – principally to make it better than what he thought was good enough in the first place.

ERNIE: He always said he had an ambition to write a routine that was absolutely perfect in one go. It's never happened with us, but that doesn't stop his being the tops.

ERIC: Actually, I think it *has* happened a couple of times with Eddie. It happened once with Sid and Dick.

ERNIE: It's a question of standards. Our ideas of perfection may not be somebody else's. We set our own standards. It doesn't mean we're right, but we think we are. The hardest thing to find is good business – funny business, a new way of lighting a cigar, a funny way of pouring a cup of tea. It has to be done so well that it becomes a natural instinct.

ERIC: You're talking about my sex life again, aren't you? But you're right. Can I just qualify that by saying that we only know what is good for Morecambe and Wise? I don't know what is good for Cannon and Ball. I don't know what is good for Little and Large, I never knew what was good for Jimmy and Ben, Laurel and Hardy, or Abbott and Costello. There have been times when we have completely abandoned a script, not just one of Eddie's, but one by Sid and Dick or which we've done ourselves.

Ernie can come in one morning, all bubbling, and say, 'I've got a great idea', and we all look at him as if he's dropped dead. He expounds his theory and it is about as funny as a cry for help. When it doesn't work, we all get slightly depressed, mutter 'bloody hell' a few times and then decide we all have to think harder.

ERNIE: But when we get a really good idea, we are thrilled to bits

120

with it. The thing is, you mustn't destroy somebody simply because they think of a bad idea.

To be fair, one does sometimes persuade the other. Sometimes Eric has an idea which I don't like. We let it lie fallow for a time and then I might come back to it. In that case, we build it up and end up with both of us positive that it's great.

ERIC: Very rarely does it go the other way round – that we squash a previously good idea. There's always the thought at the back of our minds that if it had been a good idea before, it must still be one now.

ERNIE: It's a sort of gut feeling. In 1970 I had an idea to show pictures of all the guest stars and everybody else on the show when they were children, as if it were an edition of. *This Is Your Life*. We would get a big star on the show, and show him as a six-month-old boy on a tiger-skin rug. We would show Glenda Jackson as a little girl. These would be real pictures. There would be Elton John as a little boy and the *Dad's Army* people as young men. We would put the producer on as, say, Franker.stein. The pictures would be in black-and-white. But Tom Sloan, who used to be head of BBC Light Entertainment, came round to have a look at the show and cut them all out. He said, 'It's in colour. We don't want black-and-white pictures.' We cut them out, but we did it all again five years later and nobody said anything. Tom Sloan wasn't there any more. He just didn't see it. Sometimes we feel like saying, 'You do your job and we'll do ours.'

ERIC: Just get us more money.

ERNIE: But we've always done those little extras. And we always will.

Of course, to the television companies it is all a question of ratings and it's in the companies that our money is. They get the ratings, we get the money.

ERIC: Of course, we worry about ratings. I often think that the whole ratings game will change when video finally takes over. People will say, 'Well, I'll watch that, and tape the other show.' What's going to happen to ratings then? It would be much easier for the artists if there weren't any at all.

ERNIE: But not to the executives, although they never know what we're doing till they see the shows screened. They might occasionally have a sneak look if they want to, but I've never met any executive who in my opinion can give a definite answer or who could say, 'That was a great show which is going to be an enormous success.' Even we can't say that.

We had trouble with our Christmas 1979 show, the first after Eric's operation. What we didn't know was the the BBC were going to put on *The Sting* in competition. That knocked us down the ratings position. It doesn't matter if we've got the best show in the world – which is also one of the greatest shows we've ever done – if nobody's watching it, you can forget about it. I've heard that half the trouble was that the various independent television companies were unable to agree on what they showed before we came on, so the timings were all wrong. And instead of beginning our show just before *The Sting*, they let us go on thirty minutes after it had started – so that *The Three Musketeers* could finish. Nobody was going to stay with a film like that if they could watch *The Sting*, a super Hollywood picture – nor were they going to switch off *The Sting* after half an hour just to watch Morecambe and Wise. If ITV want to get the viewers, they've got to get all that together. They need to have a picture in opposition to the BBC's which can be a springboard for the programme that follows – like ours.

ERIC: They've got to work for the Bond film or whatever they're showing, no matter what it costs, and then for Morecambe and Wise. If they've got a Bond film followed by us and there are eighteen million viewers watching that, it doesn't matter what the BBC have – *The Sound of Music* or *Gone with the Wind* – nobody's going to switch off.

Actually that 1979 Christmas show broke all our usual rules. It was completely off the cuff – or at least ninety per cent of it was. We asked David Frost if he would like to interview us, but we said, 'Please don't tell us what you're going to say.' We knew that Des was coming on and that Glenda would be there, but we only worked out the songs. I don't think there's a recipe in that for a future show, though. We have got to go on and entertain people and work it at.

ERNIE: That year was totally different. Eric couldn't physically work. The one skilled routine number we had – the pussy cat – we did in sections, so there wasn't too much strain on him.

ERIC: Frankly, I just didn't know whether I could still do anything properly or if the people were going to turn round and say, 'Oh dear, how sad . . .' Fortunately, it didn't turn out like that. I still get letters saying, 'You shouldn't have done that jumping up and down', or 'You shouldn't have sprung over the settee as you did'. But then there were the other letters, saying, 'My husband's going into hospital this week for the same operation that you had and he was thrilled to see you jump over the settee. It's given him a lot of confidence.'

ERNIE: We want the public to get their confidence back, too – so as not to worry about what Eric does and to watch the shows simply as shows. We don't want sympathy in people's minds.

ERIC: And even if that show hadn't worked out, I wouldn't have packed it all in.

ERNIE: We'd probably have done bank raids.

ERIC: Or a different style of TV show.

ERNIE: We shall overcome ... I will return.

ERIC: It's the greatest business in the world.

12

At Last

ERNIE: If I were to die now, my epitaph would be 'I was still on my way to Hollywood'. Call it insecurity if you like, I feel you haven't made it to the top unless you've made it in America. That's why we have so much enthusiasm for our shows playing in the States. Although we used to do the Ed Sullivan shows and had our own series, *Piccadilly Palace*, we've never had the same following as we have in England.

Believe it or not, there's a language problem. They've always wanted us to call lifts 'elevators' and pavements 'sidewalks'. Our British audience would never accept that. Perhaps America is now ready for lifts and pavements.

ERIC: I don't even want to think about working in America.

ERNIE: He doesn't want to go, he's not interested.

ERIC: Taking the shows to America in 1980 didn't represent the biggest slice of money we ever had, although the price was all right. We received a percentage on the deal between the BBC and Time-Life for fifty *Morecambe and Wise Shows* which were repackaged into seventy half-hour-long shows.

ERNIE: They were broadcast five nights a week on local networks all over the country, from New York to Los Angeles. But it's the bottom rung of the ladder; we aren't yet on the major networks.

ERIC: First reactions were very encouraging though. We've received letters from new fans three thousand miles away. Marvellous!

ERNIE: They got the shows very reasonably, especially since they were showing their programmes five nights a week. Our hope is that everybody will get to know our faces, a mass audience will follow us, and we could start to advertise things. We could even get a film script. That's what we really want. We now have two films in mind, including the one that's virtually written. If we were big they'd be pushing money under the door.

ERIC: The trouble is, we are competing with thirteen other American channels. We were being shown in places like Nevada where it is ninety-per cent desert.

ERNIE: Yes, and it's one thing getting people to view you and another getting them to like you.

ERIC: Even if nobody saw the series, it was on. That's what matters.

ERNIE: The deal started as a result of a trip we made to Jersey for a big charity affair at Billy Butlin's place. Afterwards, at the dinner, I was talking to a *Daily Express* journalist who asked about our appearing in the States. 'The BBC can't sell us, we did better while we were with Lew Grade,' I said. 'We did the Ed Sullivan show, on which we did very well, and Lord Grade sold us as *Piccadilly Palace*. But the BBC can't. It's hopeless, just a waste of time.'

He printed it in the William Hickey column. It was a bit stinging as far as BBC Enterprises were concerned. But one thing led to another and eventually they told me, 'We *have* been trying to sell you, but the Americans can't understand what Eric says.'

I wasn't taking it lying down. I told them in no uncertain terms that I thought the time was ripe *now* for selling us. I offered to help them pick out the shows that I thought would do well in the States. Eventually, people came over from Time-Life and I gave them more or less a list of things that I thought would do well across the Atlantic. I think that after the success of the Monty Python and Benny Hill shows they were willing to take the risk. Ours is considered 'adult humour' – Benny Hill is, too; they can't show him at prime time, seven or eight o'clock. I knew that someone like Glenda Jackson had got to be a success and that the Caesar and Cleopatra routine was a natural. If there were any references in it which the Americans thought were a bit too English, they could either snip them out or let them go – after all, we watch American shows in which they talk about freeways. We know what they mean without having to jump for a dictionary.

ERIC: We've said we wouldn't revise any of the scripts or re-do anything. We certainly weren't going to take out words like 'cobblers'. If they don't want it, they don't want it. They've come in too late to change our style.

ERNIE: We stayed in England because we didn't want to change our image. We worked on the home market because we're English comedians. We didn't want to do what Tom Jones and Engelbert Humperdinck had done.

ERIC: That's another story. They're not comics, but they get big laughs from me.

ERNIE: If I can do anything to promote our shows in America, I will.

ERIC: Ernie may be the business expert in our partnership, but we always talk things over together. So far, when talking over the question of going to America, it ends with my saying I'm not going. But if there was a very good chance of our getting a better series through my going over, I'd do it – under duress. I'm not a born traveller anyway. I'm not over-keen on seeing far-away places like Ernie is.

On the BBC deal with Time-Life everything was pre-arranged and a trip wouldn't have made any difference at all. We wouldn't have made any money out of it, just a free trip. To me, that's hard work. I've got to the point where I don't need that sort of thing any more.

ERNIE: I enjoy it, it's business.

ERIC: Other people will take credit for getting our shows on in the States, but ninety-nine per cent of the work was done by Ernie. I was lying in hospital and he went out and did it.

ERNIE: I think opportunity finally knocked. We were coming in on the wave that launched Benny Hill and Monty Python.

ERIC: Fortunately, America has an English kick about once every twelve years and in 1979 they had just launched another one. A new slot was created on television by means of syndication and they need all the material, all the shows they can get a hold of. It must be easier – and probably cheaper – to get seventy *Morecambe and Wise Shows* than having to make them up. And we *almost* sound as if we are talking English to them. It was a matter of convincing the Americans that we had what they wanted to see.

ERNIE: It's the sort of thing that should have happened ten years before.

126

ERIC: Somebody told us that years ago.

ERNIE: It's a bit late in life now.

ERIC: We can't really take it on now, the harassment of America. We couldn't take the pace. I really think that if we had taken off ten years ago in America, we might both have been dead by now in that rat race. And I couldn't have afforded the cost of my operation over there.

ERNIE: The thing is that we are not even contemplating financial gain; it's just the achievement of going out, as a regular series, in America, that we feel pleased about.

ERIC: Even a medium success won't bring us stardom in the American sense of the word. Benny Hill can't work in Las Vegas yet; neither can we.

ERNIE: That's the yardstick.

ERIC: We can't say we want $100,000 a night in Las Vegas, and yet there are people topping the bills in Vegas that we've never heard of over here. It's purely and simply that America is the centre of show business and they don't care about what happens elsewhere. There are, in fact, people in America who work only Vegas and the Catskills, Atlantic City and Lake Tahoe. The hardest thing for us to do now is to stay where we are. And there's no such thing as a guarantee. We have nothing to sell when it's all finished; we haven't a factory which we'll sell for half a million dollars, only a suit which we wore in a sketch.

ERNIE: We're marking time now, just looking for opportunities and products. But we can't follow through like we could have done ten years ago. We couldn't start taking on twenty-six brand new television shows for the States. If, though, they came to us and said we could do whatever we wanted in America, that would be another matter.

ERIC: But it's up to them. I don't want to start again at my age and say, 'Let's work entirely for America.' I don't want to know about that. If they accepted us as they have accepted Benny Hill, then I'd be thrilled, but I don't want to go over there to do it. They're no better than we are as performers, but I don't want to travel six thousand miles to start proving it.

ERNIE: It depends entirely on whether or not you want to do it.

ERIC: And I don't. I've never enjoyed working in America. I don't see America as the goal to end all goals for us, the way Ernie does.

Let's put it the other way, Ernie: you've been offered a film, by yourself, in Rome - in an Italian film where, for argument's sake, you play the part of a small cowboy, a killer. Would you do that and forget about Hollywood?

ERNIE: If it interested me enough, I suppose. Yes.

ERIC: But if you were offered a bad part in Hollywood, you would still want to go there, wouldn't you?

ERNIE: Well, any part in a film could move you on to something else, couldn't it?

ERIC: What you like is the idea of walking around a swimming-pool with a dry Martini in your hand.

ERNIE: That was what I was sold on in the first place, when I was a kid.

ERIC: But you've been there - you've done it two or three times.

ERNIE: Yes, but I'm still on the way.

ERIC: But doing what?

ERNIE: I don't know.

ERIC: I can't see myself there. I can only be me and I ain't been invited. We're the best double act that this country has ever seen in *all* its existence - Morecambe and Wise, for heaven's sake - and we still haven't been invited to Hollywood, so there's something that we aren't doing right! There is no chance and never has been for Morecambe and Wise to succeed in Hollywood, because we're not that type of performer. Had you been a single, you might have got there as a younger man, but I don't see any way that you are going to get there now.

ERNIE: That's what dreams are made of.

ERIC: But we've made a dream. The dream came true. It's here. What you're going for is the meringue on the pie.

ERNIE: What I'm saying is, I was going to be another Mickey Rooney ...

ERIC: But you became Ernie Wise. Isn't being the first Ernie Wise better than being another Mickey Rooney?

ERNIE: Yes, now. But I'm talking about when I was twelve.

ERIC: But you're still talking about 'when I get to Hollywood' as if Hollywood was the big answer. But it isn't, is it? Look what it did for Bruce Forsyth. Nothing!

ERNIE: It's just travelling and having somewhere to go, that's all.

ERIC: I often wonder how far we can now go. Perhaps we have

reached the peak already – apart from America, which I am not interested in, or scoring at the Montreux Festivals and things like that, which I feel are too much of an effort. If I'm going to do anything, I've got to do it here. For my health's sake. I've got to carry on doing it here, making my living here. But how far along the road are we really today? Are we at the peak now or have we got another year, another four years or another ten years? Our 1980 series was top of the ratings over six weeks – that is, every show we did – which must prove something, but in ten years' time I shall be sixty-four. Have you ever laughed at a 64-year-old man?

ERNIE: There is Bob Hope. Jack Benny was eighty plus when he died, working almost to the end, and he was hilarious. George Burns is eighty-four, marvellous.

ERIC: Specialized, mind you. When you put all those into a unit, they wouldn't grab an audience if they were in this country. Now at sixty-four, would we have the same appeal and the same size audience that we do now? Would we grab eight million viewers or ten million viewers?

ERNIE: There's nobody else going to do what we do, the way we do it.

ERIC: Yes. Nobody did anything better than the things Laurel and Hardy did. It was their own style. Look at a Laurel and Hardy film made in 1934. It's hilarious. But see a film they made in 1954 and you won't laugh half as much.

ERNIE: Audiences' attitudes change as time goes on.

ERIC: But I don't want the audiences' attitude to change. I don't want Laurel and Hardy to get old when I see their pictures. That's why I feel that if we play our cards right we're never off television. They don't notice how much hair I'm losing, but it wouldn't be the same if they hadn't seen me since 1956 when all my hair was there. The Eric and Ernie they know are the Eric and Ernie of today. They don't think in terms of our 1956 selves.

Even so, I do think that we have now reached the stage in our careers when we have to consider how far we go before retiring. But one thing's for certain: we *would* continue working, if only for our own sake.

ERNIE: No, I don't think that's true. If the public weren't interested and they didn't want us any more, we would disappear over the skyline like all good cowboys did in the best Westerns. I wouldn't want to bore people, and if they didn't want us any more, then that's it.

ERIC: But it wouldn't be an overnight decision. It's going to take a couple of years for us to fade away. Then we either say, 'Well, that's it', or we go into some other form of show business. We might say, 'Okay, for the next two years we'll do nothing but theatres', back to the bank raids and clear up. We'd make more money doing that than we're making now. Then we would finish it.

ERNIE: But bank raids depend entirely on the amount of business that comes in. If we started with six theatres and they sold out, as they did in the old days, then fine. But if not? The speed of the sell-out has always reflected the size of the popularity. We wouldn't go on to perform to half-empty houses. Half-full ones, yes, perhaps. I don't think we would want to tour if there was no business. I've always said that if they were bored, that is when I would pack it in. I see no reason to change my mind now.

ERIC: Yes. I think I would pack in all the shows tomorrow, but not show business. I think we could easily get ourselves a quiz show of some description like *Call My Bluff*. It would earn us a few bob a year and keep our names in front of the public. But we're not ready for it yet. There's never an end to a series. It's always the next show, the next series. We might take three months off, but all the time we are thinking of the next show and stockpiling ideas for the next series. Except when I'm actually on the Thames fishing. Work cannot interfere with that.

ERNIE: Years ago we did nothing else but work.

ERIC: Now when I go fishing I only think about fishing, I never think about show business.

If show people are not careful, and we could be just as susceptible as anyone else, they get on that treadmill to oblivion. And for what reason? Okay we're making a lot of money, but we're paying a lot of tax. So we only make it to pay tax. But I think we have got it about right. To me, the beauty of show business in this country is that I can work three months and fish nine months. And people love us, they don't just accept us. They don't just think we're funny. It's not that they say we can't do any wrong, but because of that love they will accept most of the stuff that we do. In the States, it would be entirely different. They hate failure there. If we had a bad show in America they would turn round and say, 'Well, let's forget them.'

Over here, the reaction would be: 'You've got to give them a chance. Eric hasn't been well.'

ERNIE: Quite seriously, we know that if Thames and the other television companies told us, 'We don't want you any more, you're not a large enough proposition', we could go out and perform tomorrow.

ERIC: We'd work in pubs.

ERNIE: We wouldn't want to, but we could.

ERIC: We could give you one and a half hours – it might be high-class rubbish, but it's an hour and a half.

ERNIE: Gregory Peck can't do that, unless he goes out and does readings – which Charles Laughton did.

ERIC: He read my meter wrong.

ERNIE: We could still get up and perform, we're still performers, we're still our own motivation. But as we go on, the style of the *Morecambe and Wise Show* changes. I think the next step will be a complete show based on our flat. We can't do the dancing any more. We would still do the occasional music bit, but it might turn into a Hancock and James situation or be like Amos and Andy in America.

ERIC: It's *The Odd Couple* again.

ERNIE: *The Odd Couple* is the perfect example of what Eric and I could be. The two divorced fellows living together in the flat. Neil Simon said it all and he said it in *The Sunshine Boys* too. That's us. A couple of Sunshine Boys.

ERIC: But, Sunshine, our success is based on our ability to know our limitations. People say to us, 'You could go out there and you could read the telephone book and it would be hilarious', but you just *can't* go out there and be funny.

ERNIE: They don't remember the good or the bad bits, they just say, 'They've gone off', and you've had it. It's as simple as that.

ERIC: You need to have talent not just to entertain but to recognize when the material is right for you. We're in a very unique position because we've done the Star and Garter, we've done the Palladium, and we've done everything in between. To be truthful, what we'd like to do most is simply to keep where we are. They're the operative words, to keep where we are – in television.

Television is more important today than movies used to be. A lot of people today have two sets, and I like to thank them for allowing me into their bedrooms while I watch. But we can't do without television to stay where we are, and writers to keep us there.

ERNIE: There's only one danger with television. We can lose physical contact with the public.

ERIC: No, I disagree. You start losing contact with your public when your ratings don't come up. It all depends on ratings. We will never alter the way we work, whether we're dying on our feet or whether we're an enormous success – because we can't. You're not a good enough actor and neither am I. We can't just change. The fact is that the public do not accept what is being offered to them by us or anyone unless it is good.

ERNIE: And we can only do what we can put into our own idiom. We are what we are.

ERIC: And we know how very lucky we are to be a success.

ERNIE: When the fun goes out of it and we don't enjoy it any more, that is when we stop. People always say, 'You don't perform. You play.' And we do. While we're entertaining the public, we play as well.

ERIC: But we don't just work for the fun of it. Cash is still important. We add a 'd' to the fun and make it f-u-n-d-s and not just fun. Quite seriously, Ernie and I could earn a million pounds a year now – we could even earn a million each if we wanted to.

ERNIE: But we'd have to work every night.

ERIC: If we were fit enough.

ERNIE: Money is not sufficiently important for us to be working every night. Making an audience laugh and like us is magic. We can feel the warmth coming from that audience. It's a very special feeling – something you just can't buy.

ERIC: There's no answer to that.